REFORM,
REBELLION
and the
HEAVENLY WAY

Founder and First Great Leader of Ch'ŏndogyo,
Ch'oe Che-u
(Official Ch'ŏndogyo Portrait)

REFORM, REBELLION
and the
HEAVENLY WAY

Benjamin B. Weems

The Association For Asian Studies: Monographs and Papers, No. XV
Delmer M. Brown, *editor*

THE UNIVERSITY OF ARIZONA PRESS
TUCSON   ARIZONA

The publication of this volume has been made possible by a generous grant to The Association For Asian Studies by the Ford Foundation.

First printing, 1964
Second printing, 1966

PREFACE

This monograph is a revision of a thesis written under the direction of Dr. Stefan T. Possony in the Department of Government of Georgetown University in partial fulfillment of the requirements for the degree of Master of Arts, conferred in 1955. The author is indebted to the Georgetown Committee on Publications for permission to publish this material. The writer is deeply grateful for the continuing assistance and encouragement given by the staff of the Division of Orientalia of the Library of Congress. Mr. Key P. Yang, Specialist on Korea in the Division of Orientalia, has been particularly helpful. In addition to rendering enthusiastic cooperation in his official capacity, he has given freely of his own time and performed invaluable service in the translation and evaluation of Korean and Japanese language materials. The author has had the benefit of many constructive comments by his brother, Dr. C. N. Weems of New York University, who has reviewed the entire manuscript in the light of his own extensive research on Korean history and international relations. The author, of course, assumes full responsibility for the work, including in particular all judgments expressed.

In this study, all dates are rendered according to the Western calendar; those dates which in the original appear in terms of the lunar calendar have been converted in accordance with *A Sino-Western Calendar for Two Thousand Years, 1-2000 A. D.* by Hsueh Chung-san and Ouyang Yi (Changsha: The Commercial Press, Ltd., 1940). In the romanization of Korean words, the study follows the McCune-Reischauer System, as amended by the Library of Congress to provide for hyphenization of given names.

MONOGRAPHS AND PAPERS OF THE ASSOCIATION FOR ASIAN STUDIES

Contents

Illustrations

INTRODUCTION

Ch'ŏndogyo, the "Religion of the Heavenly Way," played a significant role in the development of Korean nationalism and in Korea's fight for independence. Although it began in 1860 as a religious reform movement, Ch'ŏndogyo early acquired a strongly political tone. It is in the field of political thought and action (largely inspired, to be sure, by a quasi-religious ideology) that the movement made its principal impact. The specific character and significance of Ch'ŏndogyo varied in accordance with changing conditions during the three important periods in Korea's national life when the movement was active.

The first period (1860-1905) was characterized by the extreme incompetence and venality of the declining Korean monarchy (Yi dynasty) and by struggles among rival foreign powers for dominance in the country. Tonghak (Eastern Learning), as Ch'ŏndogyo was known during these years, was a reform movement directed against the social, economic, and political abuses of the time. It remained sectarian, however, without support from other reformist elements in Korea. This stage in the life of Ch'ŏndogyo was climaxed by the Tonghak Rebellion of 1894 which seriously threatened to overthrow the existing Korean Government. Moreover, by furnishing a pretext for the entry of Chinese and Japanese troops into the Korean peninsula, the rebellion served as a spark that set off the Sino-Japanese War of 1894-1895.

The second period was that of Japanese control of Korea, beginning in 1905 with the establishment of the Japanese protectorate and ending with the defeat of Japan in 1945. During this phase, Ch'ŏndogyo abandoned the use of force, and, while retaining the character of a domestic reform movement, redirected its reformist activities toward the achievement of Korean independence from Japanese control. The highlight was the nation-wide, nonviolent independence uprising of 1919, actively participated in by Christians, Buddhists, and the Korean public generally, but organized and financed largely by Ch'ŏndogyo. Subsequently, as Japanese suppressive measures became increasingly severe, Ch'ŏndogyo of necessity went underground as a political organization, but was able to continue to operate overtly as a religious cult and as an agency fostering ethical and economic self-improvement.

The third period, from the end of World War II in 1945 until the invasion of South Korea in 1950, was characterized by the disastrous division of Korea and the progressive development of two mutually hostile economic-political systems in the country. During these postwar years, Ch'ŏndogyo attempted to play the role of a middle-of-the-road movement advocating the establishment of an independent, "Korean style" government based upon political and economic policies bearing similarities to those of both Marxism and Western democracy, but aligned neither with the Soviet Bloc nor with the Western World. In this attempt, Ch'ŏndogyo demonstrated that its political and economic programs were not sufficiently virile to withstand the sharp conflict between the Communist and anti-Communist political forces in Korea. In North Korea, the movement gradually lost its identity through progressive accommodation to the Soviet-sponsored Communist regime. In South Korea, Ch'ŏndogyo became impotent as a result of its own internal factionalism and the overpowering force of anti-Communist nationalism.

The Tonghak phase of Ch'ŏndogyo (1860-1905) bears interesting similarities to the Taip'ing movement in China (1850-64). The political, economic, and social conditions which gave rise to the two movements were generally the same. In both Korea and China, a corrupt and declining monarchy was controlled by a minority ruling element. In both countries, this elite placed upon the vast majority of the people an extremely oppressive burden of class obligations, taxation, and official "squeeze," and left them without legal protection either of their personal safety or of their meager earnings. Each of the two movements had its genesis from alleged supernatural revelations to its founder. Each, also, found initial expression as a religious cult which bore superficial resemblances to Christianity and which preached a message of social reform appealing to the oppressed common people. Moreover, both Tonghak and Taip'ing, while retaining their reformist religious dogma as an ideological base, developed into dissident political movements with sufficient strength to threaten the existence of the ruling monarchies. The Taip'ing actually acquired effective governmental control of a major part of China for more than a decade, but collapsed completely when driven from power. The Tonghak movement, on the other hand, failed to achieve governmental status, as a result of the defeat of the Tonghak Rebellion of 1894. Tonghak, however, was able to survive this defeat, redirect its activities, and achieve perhaps greater success later as a nonviolent independence movement against Japanese imperialism.[1]

A delegation which the Korean Government sent to China to investigate the Taip'ing uprising was apparently primarily disturbed by the evidence of Western religious influence upon the movement. At any rate, one Korean historian has reported that, as a result of the concern shown by the Korean Government over the Taip'ing developments, the Tonghak founder, Ch'oe Che-u, became sensitive to the Western influence exerted by Catholicism in Korea.[2] However, despite the fact that Ch'oe was familiar with the Taip'ing movement, all available evidence indicates that the social and political motivations of the Tonghak movement were indigenous to Korea. The eclectic doctrine of Ch'oe Che-u

---

[1]For details on the Taip'ing Rebellion, see M. E. Cameron, T. H. D. Mahoney, and G. E. McReynolds, *China, Japan and the Powers* (New York: Ronald Press, 1952), pp. 206-218; also Arthur W. Hummel (ed.), *Eminent Chinese of the Ch'ing Period (1644-1912)* (Washington: Govt. Printing Office, 1943), Vol. 1, pp. 361-369; Vol. II, pp. 655-658: Vol. II, pp. 751-756.

[2]Kang Chae-ŏn, "Chōsen ni Okeru Hōken Taisei no Kaitai to Nōmin Sensō [The Breakdown of the Feudal System and the Farmers' Struggle in Korea], *Rekishigaku Kenkyū* [Journal of Historical Studies] (Tokyo: Iwanami Shōten), No. 7, July 1954, pp. 11-12.

was also distinctly Korean, although many of the component religious concepts, which had long been accepted in Korea, had not originated there.[3]

Despite the noteworthy part played by Ch'ŏndogyo in the politics and international relations of Korea for almost a century, no analytical political study of the movement as a whole has ever before been made. Korean and Japanese scholars have done, and continue to do, very useful historical research on certain aspects of the Ch'ŏndogyo movement, particularly the Tonghak Rebellion of 1894. Christian missionaries who have written on Ch'ŏndogyo have dealt almost exclusively with its importance as a native religious cult competing with Christianity. Other Western writers have written on incidents involving Ch'ŏndogyo (notably the Tonghak Rebellion and the 1919 independence uprising) which were of general historical interest. The present study, utilizing both Oriental and Western language sources, attempts to give continuity to the movement and to analyze its objectives, techniques, and accomplishments in the perspective of parallel developments in Korea and the Far East.

Benjamin B. Weems

---

[3]Yi Ton-hwa, *In Nae Ch'ŏn ŭi Yoŭi* [Essentials of *In Nae Ch'ŏn*] (Seoul: Ch'ŏndogyo Central Hq., 1924), p. 30. See also Charles A. Clark, *Religions of Old Korea* (New York: Revell, 1932), p. 165.

CHAPTER I
THE SETTING

Korea has a documented history of more than two thousand years. Although recurrently beset by depredations and invasions by stronger neighbors, the nation for some sixteen centuries demonstrated notable recuperative powers and enjoyed extensive periods of enlightened monarchical government and significant cultural achievements. The last such period of greatness under the Korean monarchy extended for about the first century and half of the Yi Dynasty (established in 1392), spanning the age of the great discoverers in the West.

This creative era in Korea came to a close near the end of the reign of King Chungjong (1505-1544). At about this time, the Confucian elite, who were the mainstay of Yi Dynasty government and society, saw no more worlds to conquer, began to bicker over artificial doctrinal issues, and instituted a bitter factional competition for the spoils of office. The resultant undermining of Korea's governmental and social structure weakened the nation at the very time when it needed all its former strength to resist new foreign encroachments.

The massive Japanese invasion under Hideyoshi began in 1592. The invaders were finally driven back in 1598 by the remarkable exploits of Korean Admiral Yi Sun-sin in destroying the Japanese fleet, and also by belated military assistance from the Chinese Emperor, the mutually recognized "elder brother" of the King of Korea. The Hideyoshi invasion had, however, wreaked virtually complete devastation throughout Korea and had seriously aggravated the demoralization of the Korean people. Further misfortune came about thirty years later, when the Manchus deposed the Ming as the rulers of China. The Manchus (Ch'ing Dynasty) invaded Korea and demanded the annual payment of tribute by the Korean King in recognition of the legitimacy of the Ch'ing succession to the Ming. The King acceded to the Manchu demands in 1637.[1]

---

[1]Homer B. Hulbert, *The History of Korea* (2 vols.; Seoul; Methodist Publ. House, 1905), Vol. II, *passim*. Clarence N. Weems, Jr., "The Korean Reform and Independence Movement" (Unpublished Ph.D. dissertation, Faculty of Political Science, Columbia University, 1954), pp. 10-13. See also Harold M. Vinacke, *A History of the Far East in Modern Times* (4th ed.; New York: Crofts, 1941), pp. 123-144 and Horace N. Allen, "The Awakening of Korea," in George H. Blakeslee (ed.), *China and the Far East* (New York: Crowell, 1910), pp. 369-396. For a detailed presentation of the "elder brother" principle in Sino-Korean relations during the period under review, see M. Frederick Nelson, *Korea and the Old Orders in Eastern Asia* (Baton Rouge: Louisiana State Univ. Press, 1945), *passim*. For details on relations between Korea and the Manchu (Ch'ing) Dynasty, see Seoul Taehak Kuksa Yŏn'gu-sil [Korean History Research Center, Seoul National University], *Kuksa Kaesŏl* [Outline of Korean History] (Seoul: Hongmungwan, 1952), pp. 483-484.

From that time—during the reign of Louis XIII—until 1876, when modern Japan successfully demanded that Korea establish diplomatic relations with foreign nations, Korea maintained itself in a state of almost complete isolation from outside influences. Its once vigorous political, social and cultural institutions became stagnant, and were perverted by ruthless, avaricious ruling elements whose only concern was to acquire or maintain personal power.[2]

Internal Conditions in Nineteenth Century Korea

Ch'ŏndogyo, which was founded in the middle part of the nineteenth century (under the name of Tonghak), received its impetus principally from men whose families had long been out of favor with the ruling class. There were certain basic political-economic-social factors which impelled such men to develop and give expression to new and potentially revolutionary ideas at this time.[3]

Korean political life was so dominated by a highly stratified class system that only certain privileged elements had an opportunity to be raised to official status. This status could be acquired only through taking the *Kwagŏ* (state examinations for the civil or military service), and only members of certain families of already established social position were able to qualify for the examinations. Once a qualified candidate had passed the state examination, he was eligible for a government position and for membership in the *yangban* class (nobility). At the next social level below the *yangban* were the *chung'in* (middle people) class and also the sons of *yangban* fathers and concubines. These two groups were excluded from taking the civil and military examinations and from holding civil and military positions in the government. They were allowed to hold government positions only in technical and professional fields which were looked down upon by the *yangban*. Eligibility for such positions was acquired by a special state examination called *ch'uije* (selection of the skilled), in the fields of medicine, law, interpreting, astronomy (including mathematics), and art. Government positions were thus divided roughly into two categories: one for the *yangban,* and the other for the technicians or professionals.[4] Despite the fact that the *chung'in* class was looked down upon, its members had an opportunity to manipulate or accumulate property, and also had access to new intellectual influences. The *yangban*, on the other hand, became the slaves of their own orthodox neo-Confucian doctrine. *Chung'in* interpreters who accompanied the official Korean missions to the Chinese court were the persons primarily responsible for bringing Catholicism into Korea

---

[2]Yi Sang-guk, *Hanguk Munhwa Sa Kaegwan* [Outline of Korean Cultural History] (Seoul: Hyŏndaesa, 1955), pp. 415 ff.

[3]Han U-gŭn and Kim Ch'ŏl-chun, *Kuksa Kaeron* [General Discussion of Korean History] (Seoul: Myŏnghaktang, 1954), pp. 344-352.

[4]Kyŏngguk Taejŏn [The Great Administrative Code] (Seoul: Korean Government General, 1934), p. 156. Also, W. H. Wilkinson, *The Corean Government: Constitutional Changes, July 1894 to October 1895* (London: P. S. King and Son, 1897), *passim.*

from China. This was the avenue through which Ch'oe Che-u, the founder of Tonghak, became informed on Catholic doctrine.[5]

The Korean privileged class, from which the ruling elements came, had been established on the basis of the Confucian principle of the primacy of literary achievement. By the nineteenth century, this class was maintained and expanded through heredity and marriage. By the middle of the nineteenth century, the number of government positions was insufficient to accommodate the expanding privileged class. This condition led to increasingly bitter competition among *yangban* factions for a monopoly of government position and political power. When the *Noron* faction was victorious, the displaced *yangban* elements became a major source of disaffection and intrigue against the government.[6]

Land (the only dependable source of revenue) was, under the Korean monarchy, owned by the state. The land was assigned to government officials and leased by them to tenant farmers who cultivated it and made payment in kind both to the landlord and to the government. Most *yangban* during the 19th century continued to follow the practice of retaining possession of the land after retirement from office and of passing the title on to their sons. The *yangban* also abused their power position to acquire increased land holdings which were seldom recorded. Consequently, tax in kind to the government progressively decreased. The government attempted to raise the needed revenue by placing increased taxes on the already desperately overburdened farmers. This intense oppression of the farmers was one of the direct causes of the establishment of the Tonghak movement and the launching (in 1894) of the Tonghak Rebellion.[7]

The lower classes, which constituted the vast majority of the Korean population, were divided into the so-called *Ch'il Ch'ŏn* (Seven Lowest Official Occupations) and *P'al Ban* (Eight Socially Degraded Groups). Members of any of these depressed elements were completely at the mercy of the ruling class. The craftsmen, for instance, were required to produce goods at the demand of the ruling *yangban,* and only the leftovers were available for members of other classes. This situation was an important cause of the underdeveloped state of

[5]Yi Nŭng-hwa, *Chosŏn Kidokkyo kŭp Oegyo Sa* [History of Korean Christianity and Diplomacy] (Seoul: Kidokkyo Ch'angmunsa, 1925), II, pp. 12-13.

[6]Key P. Yang and Gregory Henderson, "An Outline History of Korean Confucianism, Part II," *The Journal of Asian Studies,* February 1959, pp. 259-275, *passim.*

[7]Yi Sang-baek, *Yijo Kŏn'guk ŭi Yŏn'gu* [A Study of the Founding of the Yi Dynasty] (Seoul: Ulyu Publishing Co., 1949), pp. 197-201; Shigada Hiroshi, "Kyurai no Chōsen Shakai no Rekishiteki Seikaku" [Old Korean Society and its Historical Characteristics], *Chōsen Gakuho,* No. 3, May 1952, p. 136. See also Yi Pyŏng-do, *Tugye Chapp'il* [Miscellaneous Writings of Tugye] (Seoul: Ilchogak, 1956), p. 90. Tugye is the penname of Professor Yi Pyŏng-do, Dean of the Graduate School, Seoul National University, and a foremost authority on Korean history.

the Korean economy and industry and gave rise to indolence and escapism.[8]

Growing Foreign Influences

At about the time that the Tonghak movement began, the influences of Christianity, Western capitalism, and international politics began to add strong external pressures to those already being felt internally. Limited contacts between Korea and the outside world had begun early in the nineteenth century, despite the fact that there were no formal foreign relations until 1876 other than the periodic missions to the Chinese court. These early, informal contacts were occasioned primarily by: (1) the shipwreck of vessels along the Korean coasts; (2) attempts by a number of foreign expeditions to open commercial and/or diplomatic relations with Korea; and (3) the activities in Korea of French Catholic priests, beginning about 1835. With respect to shipwrecks, the Korean monarchy consistently took the view that the seamen could not be blamed for such an act of fate, and that, unless they committed acts regarded as hostile, they should be assisted in returning peaceably to their countries. The commercial and diplomatic expeditions, however, were invariably looked upon as inherently hostile and were strongly suspected as being forerunners of foreign attempts to gain economic and political control of the country. This attitude was a natural outgrowth of Korea's unfortunate experiences at the hands of the Japanese and the Manchus and, at earlier periods, the Han, Sui and T'ang dynasties of China and the Mongols. This fear of foreign invaders had been intensified by Korea's long isolation and by knowledge of the humiliations which were being experienced by the once great Chinese Empire as a result of China's opening to Western influences.[9]

The evangelistic activities of the French priests were likewise suspected of having imperialistic motivations. Moreover, Christianity itself was looked

---

[8]The Seven Lowest Official Occupations *(Ch'il Ch'ŏn)* were:
   (1) *Chorye* (Official messengers)
   (2) *Najang* (Guards)
   (3) *Ilsu* (Watchmen)
   (4) *Chogun* (Oarsmen)
   (5) *Sugun* (Sailors)
   (6) *Ponggun* (Torch guards)
   (7) *Yŏkpo* (Post couriers)
The Eight Socially Degraded Groups *(P'al Ban)* were:
   (1) *Kongno* (Official slaves)
   (2) *Sano* (Private slaves)
   (3) *Ch'anggi* (Professional entertainers)
   (4) *Chŏmbok* (Fortune tellers)
   (5) *Mugyŏk* (Sorcerers and sorceresses)
   (6) *Paekchŏng* (Butchers, blacksmiths, and skilled craftsmen)
   (7) *Sŭngi* (Buddhist priests and nuns)
   (8) *Kwangdae* (Artists and acrobats)
   Korean History Research Center, Seoul National University, *Kuksa Kaesŏl* [Outline of Korean History], pp. 293-294.

[9]Han U-gŭn and Kim Ch'ŏl-chun, *op. cit.*, pp. 363-372. For details concerning Catholicism in Korea, see Charles Dallet, *Histoire de l'église de Corée*, (2 vols.; Paris: Victor Palmé, 1874); Yi Man-ch'ae, *Pyogwi P'yŏn* [Compilations of a Defense Against Heresy] (2 vols.; Seoul: Kaebyŏksa, 1931); and Gregory Henderson, "Chŏng Ta-San: A Study in Korea's Intellectual History," *The Journal of Asian Studies*, May 1957, pp. 377-386.

upon as a barbaric and dangerous doctrine. An important reason for this attitude was that conversion to Christianity was accompanied by the destruction of the Confucian ancestral tablets associated with ancestor worship. The Korean rulers regarded these tablets as symbolic of the entire Confucian system of ethics and social controls which formed the foundation of the Korean social and governmental structure.

The propagation of Christianity and the distribution of Christian literature were proscribed in 1785, and persecutions were almost continuous. Systematic, nation-wide efforts to eradicate the foreign faith were carried out in 1791, 1801, 1839, and during the period 1865-1870. Each of these brutal massacres resulted in the further growth of Korean Catholicism, after a temporary setback. In the persecutions of 1839 and 1866, French priests were executed, along with their Korean converts. In 1846, the French government sent a protest to the Korean government concerning the deaths of three French priests in the 1839 incident, and threatened punitive measures if such actions were not stopped. The Korean government, after some months' delay, rejected the French protest in a defiant reply which reflected the attitude of the Korean monarchy toward Christianity. The Korean charges against the French priests were that they had entered the country in contravention of existing Korean laws, had lived and worked incognito, and had associated with Koreans who were regarded by the government as godless and traitorous men. The Korean government, regarding these circumstances as proof that the priests had ulterior motives, declared that there had been no alternative to executing the offenders, in accordance with the law of the land. The statement further asserted that this Korean policy was well established, had been applied equally to people of other nationalities guilty of like offenses, and would not be the subject of further discussions.

This Korean government policy toward Catholicism was reintensified under the iron-handed regime of the *Taewŏngun,* the Regent, who assumed active control of the Korean government in 1864 when his twelve-year-old son succeeded to the throne. The vigorous, unenlightened *Taewŏngun* was convinced that the dangers of foreign intervention and conquest could be prevented only by a reinforcement of Korea's long-held policy of strict isolation from alien influences. The great persecution of 1865-1870 left no doubt as to the Regent's policy toward anything smacking of the hated and feared foreign religion.[10]

As has been seen, conditions in Korea in 1860 provided ample motivation for the development of a movement calling for social, economic, and political reform based on principles of equality and freedom, upon traditional Korean ethics at their best, and upon sincere patriotism and loyalty to the throne. The inequitable social and economic conditions had become intolerable to the op-

[10]Yi Nŭng-hwa, *op. cit.,* Vol. II, pp. 82-85.

pressed classes, and the entire Korean political-social-economic system was under severe strain. At the same time, the character of the ruling elements was such as to make it inevitable that they would use every available device to crush any popular movement which showed promise of seriously interfering with the systematic graft and blackmail which were primary sources of their wealth and power. These controlling elements could also be expected to suppress any indigenous movement or sentiment which was, or could be made to appear, sympathetic to the hated and feared Christianity, which they looked upon as the advance guard of foreign conquerors.

CHAPTER II
"EASTERN LEARNING" FINDS AN AUDIENCE

Against the background described in the previous chapter, Ch'ŏndogyo had its origin in the late spring of 1860 when Ch'oe Che-u, a thirty-seven-year-old scholar in southeastern Korea, allegedly received a vision in which he was commissioned by Heaven to establish a new religion. This religion would relieve the oppression of the people by creating a new way of life, or *to*, based upon the exercise of faith in God and man.[1]

Ch'oe Che-u (also known to his followers by the honorific name, "Suun") was a serious-minded, patriotic man, well educated in the Confucian Classics and in the literature of Buddhism and Taoism. He had also studied some Roman Catholic writings. He was born on December 18, 1824, at Yongdam in the vicinity of Kyŏngju, the ancient capital of the Kingdom of Silla in southeastern Korea. His father, a well-known, patriotic Confucian scholar, was one of a long line of distinguished scholars. The fact that Ch'oe Che-u's mother was a concubine had placed him in an inferior social class and made him ineligible to become a civil or military official. Moreover, his mother died when he was six years old, and he was left an orphan at the age of sixteen upon the death of his father. This background, as well as a frail physique, may have combined with his thoughtful, patriotic nature to impel him to lift himself above an unhappy environment and seek a doctrine for the salvation of his people.[2] In his Ch'ŏndogyo "Bible," *Tonggyŏng Taejŏn*,[3] Ch'oe gives his own account of how he came to found the new cult. He states that, in the year 1859, "many learned men" had come to him and asked him to explain the new doctrine which he was pondering. He described it as "Ch'ŏndogyo," the doctrine or religion of the heavenly way. When asked if his doctrine was essentially different from "Sŏhak" ("Western Learning" — a designation for Roman Catholicism), Ch'oe replied:

---

[1]Material on the founding of Ch'ŏndogyo is taken primarily from the official Ch'ŏndogyo work, *Ch'ŏndogyo Ch'ang Kŏn Sa* [History of the Origin and Establishment of Ch'ŏndogyo] (Seoul: Taedong Press, 1933), Pt. I. pp. 1-55. Corroborative sources are: Yi Sŏn-gŭn, *Hwarangdo Yŏn'gu* [A Study of Korean Knighthood] (Seoul: Haedong Cultural Press, 1949), pp. 156-164; Kim Sang-gi, *Tonghak Kwa Tonghak Nan* [Tonghak and the Tonghak Rebellion] (Seoul: Taesŏng Press, 1947), *passim.;* and Charles A. Clark, *Religions of Old Korea* (New York: Revell, 1932), pp. 144-155, 258-276.

[2]*Ch'ŏndogyo Ch'ang Kŏn Sa*, Pt. I, p. 3.

[3]This official Ch'ŏndogyo scripture, based upon Ch'oe Che-u's own writings and pronouncements, was published in 1888 by his successor, Ch'oe Si-hyŏong. The quotations used here are from *Tonggyŏng Taejŏn* Seoul: Posŏng Press, 1947).

Their purpose is similar to mine, but they do not have the truth.... My doctrine is based on the incarnation of God in man. It shows one how to control one's mind, think clearly, control one's temper, and acquire information. These foreigners have no logical sequence in their speaking, nor order in their written books, and no decorum in their worship. They only pray for selfish benefits. They have no proper spirit to inspire them in their physical life, and there is no teaching concerning the true God in their system. They have an appearance of it, but no reality. They do not have our Sacred Formula; ... and they do not really study to know God. Their differences from us are quite remarkable.[4]

It would not be right, he continued, to identify the new doctrine or teaching as "Sŏhak." "The doctrine is Heaven's Doctrine, but the teaching is Eastern Teaching, Tonghak."[5]

Ch'oe Che-u's philosophical and scholarly approach to the new doctrine is given in his own account of events leading up to his "revelation" in the spring of 1860:

After I had consulted the Chinese Book of Changes and carefully examined the reasons why my forefathers for three generations had revered God, I learned the reasons for the reverence of God by ancient scholars. On the other hand, I also learned that the people of my day had rejected reverence for God, which I sincerely deplored. If one controls oneself and constantly improves oneself, then nothing will prevent the realization of his aspirations. If one studies the Confucian teachings carefully, one will find that they contain a reasonable doctrine. My doctrine is similar to Confucianism, but there are some differences.

If one puts away doubt, a true sense of judgment will emerge. If one carefully examines the old and the new, one will find that they are mostly judged by human selfishness. I had not intended to propagate my doctrine. I exerted all my efforts in meditation.[6]

In building the doctrine of Ch'ŏndogyo, Ch'oe Che-u combined and redefined certain basic principles of Confucianism, Buddhism, and Taoism. From Confucianism, he took the concept of the five relationships (father-son, king-subject, husband-wife, elder-younger, and friend-friend); from Buddhism, the concept of heart cleansing; and from Taoism the law of cleansing the body from natural and moral filth. Ch'oe also took certain organizational and ritualistic elements from Roman Catholicism, and his writings and writings about him reflect a style and tone strangely analogous to those of the Biblical accounts of the life and teachings of Jesus Christ.[7]

An additional source of certain aspects of Ch'oe's religious system was *Ch'amwisŏl* [The Theory of Interpretation of Omens]. *Ch'amwisŏl*, which by the nineteenth century had come to exert an important influence on the Korean mind, was a combination of the spirit worship and superstitions of shamanism on the one hand and the pseudo-scientific practices of geomancy on the other. Many *Ch'amwisŏl* writings, foretelling the ultimate fall of the Yi Dynasty and making prophecies of war and other adversities, were widely known and believed during the Yi Dynasty period (1392-1910). In order to propitiate the

[4]*Tonggyŏng Taejŏn, pp. 12-13.*   [5]*Ibid.*   [6]*Ibid., pp. 26-27.*

[7]William M. Junkin, "The Tong Hak," *Korean Repository,* II (1895), p. 57. Also, Yi Ton-hwa, *In Nae Ch'ŏn ŭi Yoŭi* [Essentials of *In Nae Ch'ŏn*] (Seoul: Ch'ŏndogyo Central Hq., 1924), p. 42.

spirits which might bring these calamities, certain "magic" formulas, utilizing key words or ideographs from traditional *Ch'amwisŏl* literature, had been devised. Among these were the character combinations *KUNG-KUNG* and *UL-UL*. Also, since Korea was in a position of almost constant danger of invasion and conquest, there was a continuing feeling of uneasiness. From this feeling there developed a popular, escapist longing for a utopia.

In devising his Sacred Formula, described below, Ch'oe Che-u used the characters *KUNG* and *UL* which had appeared in the traditional *Ch'amwisŏl* formulas discussed above. Moreover, certain religious ceremonies of Tonghak (Ch'ŏndogyo) bore some similarity to those of shamanistic spirit worship, and the Tonghak practice of building altars on mountains was adopted from shamanism. Finally, Ch'oe utilized the escapist trend of the time in developing the principle, discussed later in this chapter, that sincere believers in the Tonghak doctrine would find utopia, or heaven on earth.[8]

The theoretical and ritualistic basis of Ch'ŏndogyo doctrine is embodied in the twenty-one character Sacred Formula which Ch'oe Che-u created, allegedly under divine inspiration. This Formula reads:

Infinite Energy being now within me, I yearn that it may pour into all living beings and created things.
Since this Infinite Energy abides in me, I am identified with God, and of one nature with all existence.
Should I ever forget these things, all existing things will know of it.[9]

From the Sacred Formula, Ch'oe derived the principle of *in nae ch'ŏn* (man and God are one), which is the foundation of the entire religious dogma and political philosophy of Ch'ŏndogyo. This principle means, in brief, that, potentially, man is God, but that this oneness is actually realized only as the individual exercises sincere faith in the oneness of his own spirit and body and in the universality of God. The individual must also implement this faith by harmonizing all truth into a *to*, or way of life, based upon the *in nae ch'ŏn* principle.[10] This principle is succinctly explained in Ch'ŏndogyo literature as follows:

What is the philosophical meaning of *in nae ch'ŏn*? I shall try to explain the application of the principle of *in nae ch'ŏn*, which is the basic principle of Ch'ŏndogyo, in relation to modern thinking. In brief, there are two parts to the principle of *in nae ch'ŏn*. One is philosophical and the other practical. The philosophical aspect may be divided as follows: (1) the present world and *in nae ch'ŏn*; (2) reality and *in nae ch'ŏn*; (3) pantheism and *in nae ch'ŏn*; (4) *in nae ch'ŏn* as applied to life; (5) *in nae ch'ŏn* in relation to the human senses; (6) the problem of the soul and *in nae ch'ŏn*; and (7) evolution and *in nae ch'ŏn*.

[8]Kim Sang-gi, *op. cit.*, pp. 25-58. Also, Yi Pyŏng-do, *Tugye Chapp'il*, p. 85.

[9]Clark, *op. cit.*, pp. 155-156. This translation has been checked against the original, which appears in *Tonggyŏng Taejŏn*, pp. 4-5, and *Ch'ŏndogyo Ch'ang Kŏn Sa*, Pt. I, pp. 23-26.

[10]"In Nae Ch'ŏn Yŏn'gu" [A Study of *In Nae Ch'ŏn*], a series of unsigned articles appearing in the June, July, and September, 1920 issues of *Kaebyŏk* [Creation], an official Ch'ŏndogyo periodical.

The practical aspect of *in nae ch'ŏn* is naturalism, for which modern people are yearning. Naturalism is related to the problems of equality, freedom, humanism, and justice. These are the problems which *in nae ch'ŏn* strives constantly to solve.[11]

As applied to man's relations in society, the underlying concept of *in nae ch'ŏn* is reflected in the theory of *tong kwi il che* (all life evolves toward a social oneness). This theory holds that human society is a collective, cooperative, organized body of individuals, and that the relationships of the individual to society as a whole can be likened to those of a component part of the human body to the whole body. The body as a whole coordinates all the organs of the body. The different parts function for the coordinated development of the whole body, and each part demonstrates its full capacity in order that the continuous well-being of the whole body may be achieved. Accordingly, the optimum improvement of society cannot be achieved if the development of the individual is ignored, nor can the individual develop himself to the highest degree outside of the coordinating and harmonizing influence of society. The theory holds that gradually the optimum relationships will become a reality, and all mankind will have an equal freedom of oneness within society.[12]

In the field of ethics, the *in nae ch'ŏn* principle is applied in the theory of *sa in yŏ ch'ŏn* (treat people as though they were God). *Sa in yŏ ch'ŏn* encompasses the virtues of sincerity, respect, and faith. Sincerity, in turn, is conceived of as embracing truth, diligence, and energy. Respect involves: (1) respect for heaven (that is, religious consciousness, broadly defined to include devotion to worthy causes such as the struggle for independence and social justice); (2) respect for man (that is, respect for individual character and actions, without social discrimination); and (3) respect for things (that is, a regard for the value of all things given by heaven, as in the protection of natural resources and the efficient production of goods). Faith, according to *sa in yŏ ch'ŏn,* is thought of as embracing actions of complete honesty and personal loyalty in human relations, without social discrimination.[13]

Another important theory derived from the central *in nae ch'ŏn* concept is that of *chisang ch'ŏn'guk,* (heaven on earth, or utopia). This is explained by the leading modern Ch'ŏndogyo theorist as follows:

The principle of *in nae ch'ŏn* (man and God are one) does not mean to imply that man's present mind and behavior are that of God. It means that man basically has the capacity to manifest the spirit of God. In other words, *in nae ch'ŏn* makes man a God. But this does not mean that man's present mind already possesses the mind of God.

In nae ch'ŏn was conceived in order to make this world a paradise. But this does not mean that *in nae ch'ŏn* was created because the world had already become a paradise. That is to say, man has the quality to be a God, and the present world has the quality

[11]Yi Ton-hwa, *op. cit.,* pp. 81-82; 140.

[12]*Ch'ŏndogyo Chŏngch'i Inyŏm* [Political Ideas of Ch'ŏndogyo] (Seoul: Posŏng Press, 1947), pp. 8-9.

[13]*Ibid.,* pp. 62-65.

to be a paradise. Therefore, the prime task of in nae ch'ŏn is to achieve the original purpose of man by means of developing the quality of man.

Accordingly, there are two different elements in man. The one is the natural man, and the other the divine man which is buried deeply inside the natural man. What we call the natural man is the mind we now possess, and our present behavior is not man's true nature. It is only the activity which is derived from outside customs and misrepresentations. According to the dialectical materialism of Karl Marx, man's mind does not originate from man himself, but rather is brought in from historical tradition of the outside world. Therefore, man's mind, according to Marx, is composed of factors which are. formed by the social system, custom, and habit, which were transmitted to us from many thousands of years. Hence, a new mind could be created only by breaking down or eliminating conventions and traditions.

It is very true that our mind is nothing but a crystallization of conventions and traditions. We call this contemporary mind "natural man." However, the dialectical analysis of the mind by Marxian materialism has the defect of acknowledging only one side while neglecting the other. That is to say, he knew only the natural man and did not know the creative man which is deeply hidden in the natural man. Traditions themselves originated from some vague beginning, and any sort of beginning could be regarded as creation. For instance, although our modern society is composed of traditional minds transmitted from many thousand years, the so-called tradition is an indication of the course of time. Similarly, the natural mind originated from the creative mind.[14]

The theology and philosophy incorporated in the Sacred Formula and in the doctrinal principles derived therefrom were such as to appeal to the scholarly mind. They could not have been fully grasped by the illiterate majority of the Koreans with whom Ch'oe Che-u came in contact in the propagation of his cult. The mysticism associated with ritualistic incantations of the Sacred Formula, however, was appealing to the superstitious nature of most Koreans. Moreover, in practical terms, Ch'oe's message was simply that any follower of Ch'ŏndogyo (or Tonghak, as it was then called), by exercising true faith, could acquire freedom from oppression and suffering. This message attracted large numbers of oppressed people of all economic and intellectual levels, including poor and unlettered farmers and also politically discredited members of the yangban class. Within three years after his "revelation," Ch'oe had acquired a large and devoted following throughout the provinces of southeastern and southwestern Korea.[15]

Although he went to great pains to conduct his teachings quietly and within a framework of sincere patriotism, he and his movement were the objects of continuing concern and suspicion on the part of the government. The breaking point came when an avaricious local official, attempting to make personal profit from the new organization, demanded that Ch'oe raise a large sum of money from among his followers for "special expenses" of local and county officials. Ch'oe refused to be a party to this attempted "squeeze" — one of the basic evils which had led to the founding of the Tonghak movement. The angry official

[14]Yi Ton-hwa, op. cit., pp. 199-201.

[15]Ch'ŏndogyo Ch'ang Kŏn Sa, Pt. I, pp. 36-37.

thereupon had Ch'oe imprisoned, "documenting" his action by charging Ch'oe with organizing a religion contrary to national principles and with poisoning the minds of the people.[16] This was in 1864, just as the new Regent's bloody persecution of the Catholics was getting underway. Ch'oe, in his scriptural writings, had used the words *Ch'ŏnju* and *Sangje* (meaning "Lord of Heaven" and "Superior Ruler," respectively) to refer to God. The fact that these same terms were used in Korean translations of Christian references to God formed a basis for the two damning accusations that (1) Ch'oe was proclaiming the existence of a being superior to the King (Hwangje) and (2) his doctrine was actually the same as the hated foreign doctrine, Roman Catholicism. After months of neglect and torture, Ch'oe was hanged on April 15, 1864, in Taegu at the age of forty.[17]

Ch'oe Che-u's active career had covered barely five years. In this period, he had laid down the basic Ch'ondogyo doctrine, and also the fundamental principles of loyalty to the King and noninvolvement in openly political activities — principles which became the basic guides for succeeding leaders of Ch'ŏndogyo. More than any specific principles, however, it was the magnetic force and Messianic character of the man himself which attracted people to the movement and provided it with cohesion even long after his death. The *Taesinsa* (Great Divine Teacher) inspired deep personal devotion and gave the doctrine attractiveness and meaning. The martyrdom of Ch'oe Che-u magnified, virtually to the point of deification, the high esteem in which his followers had held him during his life.[18]

The Importance of Ch'oe Che-u and his Doctrine

The Tonghak (Ch'ŏndogyo) doctrine, conceived and preached by Ch'oe Che-u, though falling short of the idealism and altruism of Christianity, was a remarkably idealistic and altruistic one as compared with any one of the Far Eastern faiths — from which it borrowed important ideas. The new doctrine was unquestionably beneficial to the many Koreans who embraced it. These people were all oppressed politically, and most of them were in desperate straits economically, as a result of the venality of the landowners and government officials. Moreover, the traditional ethical and religious systems (Confucianism and Buddhism) had little spiritual strength to offer, because they had become inextricably incorporated in the very political-economic-social system which was responsible for the abuses of the period. There was, therefore, a spiritual void which was filled by the new doctrine, with its other-worldly mysticism and its comforting and stimulating social message. The individual and group ethics in the Tonghak creed were of a high order, planting in the minds and

[16]Yi Pyŏng-do, "Tonghang-nan ŭi Yŏksa-jŏk iŭi" [Historical Significance of the Tonghak Rebellion], *Sasanggye*, No. 11, Nov., 1954, pp. 13-14.

[17]Watanabe Yŏru, *Tendōkyō to Jitenkyō* [Ch'ŏndogyo and Sich'ŏngyo] (Seoul: publ. privately, 1919), pp. 6-8. Also, *Ch'ŏndogyo Ch'ang Kŏn Sa*, Pt. I, p. 54.

[18]*Ch'ŏndogyo Ch'ang Kŏn Sa*, Pt. I, p. 54.

spirits of the faithful the seeds of an unselfish concern for one's fellow men as individuals—a concept largely lacking in the traditional Oriental religious and ethical systems.

The doctrine was essentially evolutionary, rather than revolutionary. Loyalty to the King was a cardinal Tonghak principle, as were the other traditional Confucian relationships (father-son, husband-wife, elder-younger, and friend-friend). The doctrine advocated change, but this would be, in the first instance, a change in the minds and spirits of individuals who exercised, in form and action, a deep faith in the physical and spiritual regenerative powers inherent in the basic principle of *in nae ch'ŏn* (man and God are one). These faithful, in turn, would propagate the faith in progressively widening circles until *in nae ch'ŏn* and all its social, economic, and political implications had found acceptance in the minds and spirits of all segments of Korean society, including the ruling elements.

In terms of long range potential, the implications of the doctrine were as staggering to the controlling groups in nineteenth century Korea as had been the impact of the theories of John Locke or Rousseau upon the controlling elements in eighteenth century France and England. If every sincerely faithful individual, regardless of wealth, education, or social position, was to be looked upon and treated as being equal with God, the traditional patriarchal social controls of Confucianism, the political and economic inequities perpetrated by the ruling *yangban* class, and the very class structure and factionalism which formed the basis of governmental control by cliques of self-seeking officials would all be wiped out. The fact that these changes were advocated by the Tonghaks as gradual, orderly, evolutional developments had no mitigating effect upon the violent, almost desperate hostility toward the new doctrine on the part of the intrenched *yangban,* who both as property holders and government officials, would have been the class most directly affected by any basic change. Moreover, the terminology, ritual, and social message of the Tonghak doctrine bore sufficient similarities to Christianity to lead the Korean ruling elements, who feared and hated Christianity, to adopt the same attitude toward Ch'oe Che-u's "heretical" new faith.

It is ironical that the Tonghak cult, whose founder was executed as a heretic on the grounds that he had embraced and spread the "Western Learning," later became identified as violently antiforeign in its doctrine and actions. A study of the official Ch'ŏndogyo literature covering the Tonghak period reveals no real antiforeignism in the doctrine, although Ch'oe Che-u and other Tonghak leaders did consistently protest to the government officials that the "Eastern Learning" (Tonghak) was different from, and superior to, the "Western Learning" (Sŏhak). The eradication of foreign influence, to the extent that it was a Tonghak objective, was essentially a part of the domestic political objective of removing all influences which prevented the Korean Government from operating as an independent government and according to principles which, by Tonghak standards, were just and in accord with Korea's national interests.

The Second Great Leader of Ch'ŏndogyo,
Ch'oe Si-hyŏng
(Official Ch'ŏndogyo Portrait)

CHAPTER III
THEORY PUT INTO PRACTICE

Ch'oe Che-u, the *Taesinsa*, was succeeded by a distant relative named Ch'oe Si-hyŏng, also known by the honorific name "Haewŏl". The younger Ch'oe did not inherit the title *Taesinsa* (Great Divine Teacher) which continued to be used only in reference to the revered founder, but used the somewhat more modest title of *Sinsa* (Divine Teacher). Ch'oe Si-hyŏng was born on April 16, 1827, at Kyŏngju, in the same neighborhood as his great predecessor. The boy's mother died when he was five years old and his father when he was twelve; thus he had in common with the *Taesinsa* the experience of being left an orphan at an early age. Unlike his predecessor, the *Sinsa* was a man without formal education; in fact, he himself is quoted as stating that he was incapable of writing down the *Taesinsa*'s teachings and therefore memorized them and later dictated them to others who reduced them to writing.[1] At the age of 17, he went to work in a paper factory. At the age of 35 (1862), he was converted to the Tonghak doctrine, and became a very ardent follower of Ch'oe Che-u, the *Taesinsa*. The new convert, like his Master, had visions in his zealous pursuit of the faith. In one of these visions, in the early spring of 1862, he was guided to the *Taesinsa* who commissioned him to spread the faith.

The younger Ch'oe was not only an ardent evangelist, but also an effective organizer. In the winter of 1862-63, with the approval of the *Taesinsa*, he appointed *chŏpchu*, or local group leaders, in each locality where there were Tonghak members, and inspected the religious activities of each of these groups as the *Taesinsa*'s representative. This system made the Tonghak organization more cohesive, and, by providing local channels of communication and administrative control, enabled the *Taesinsa* to make personal contact with large numbers of his followers through the *chŏpchu* in each locality.[2]

The devoutness and ability of Ch'oe Si-hyŏng, or Haewŏl, so impressed the *Taesinsa* that in the early fall of 1863, when Haewŏl had been a Tonghak member for less than two years, the latter was ordained by the *Taesinsa* as his deputy and successor. In the early spring of 1864, just before the execution of the Great Divine Teacher, Haewŏl, the new *Sinsa* (Divine Teacher), escaped to a

---

[1]*Ch'ŏndogyo Ch'ang Kŏn Sa*, Pt. II, p. 30.

[2]*Ibid.*, pp. 1-4.

retreat in the Táebaek Mountains where he was able to carry on the work of his predecessor with some assurance of evading arrest and probable death in the intensive persecution of the Tonghak sect then in progress. Later, the *Sinsa* became publicly known as "Ch'oe Pottari" ("Bundle" Ch'oe), because he never stayed in one place for more than two or three days.³

In midsummer of 1865, the *Sinsa*, after praying for forty-nine days on the mountain, began to dictate to certain of his followers the *Tonggyŏng Taejŏn* and other works of the late *Taesinsa*. (The original texts had been destroyed by fire.) Because of the continuing proscription of the Tonghak sect and the resultant necessity for Haewŏl and his followers to move about frequently to escape detection, the writings were not edited until 1880 or published until 1888.⁴

From his mountain hiding places, the *Sinsa* carried on the *Taesinsa*'s teachings, and, from time to time, made refinements of his own which applied Tonghak doctrine to practical situations. For instance, on the *Taesinsa*'s birthday in the late fall of 1865, Haewŏl preached on the subject of social equality, advocating the abolition of traditional social distinctions between the children of a first wife and those of a concubine. In other sermons, he emphasized the evils of arrogance and luxury in contemporary Korean life.⁵

The *Sinsa* formalized these religious and ethical principles in his *Nae Sudomun* (Inner Rules of Conduct), disseminated to all local Tonghak groups (*p'o*) in December, 1888. These were:

1. Respect all members of the family as you respect God: love your daughter-in-law; love your slaves just as you love your children; do not mistreat domestic animals. If you do otherwise, God will be displeased.

2. Give thanks to God when preparing rice for morning and evening meals. Cook your food with clean water.

3. Do not mix left-over rice with newly cooked rice; do not dispose of dirty water indiscriminately; do not spit indiscriminately and, if on the roadside, cover the sputum. Then God will be pleased.

4. Treat everyone as God: if a guest comes, presume that God has come; do not strike your children, because in so doing you are striking God.

5. In pregnancy, take special care of your body; be careful of your diet and of everything you do, because of the baby in your womb.

6. Do not criticize others, for in so doing you are criticizing God; do not covet anything; always be industrious.⁶

By moving about secretly, the *Sinsa* was able to exercise effective supervision through the local and regional headquarters which he himself had set up when the *Taesinsa* was still alive. The practical ability of the *Sinsa* was demonstrated by his numerous achievements in standardizing Tonghak ritual and religious observances throughout the organization.

In 1875, the *Sinsa* promulgated three regulations which had the effect of making certain Tonghak observances official and standard. These were: (1) the

---

³*Ibid.*, p.35.   ⁴*Ibid.*, p. 30.   ⁵*Ibid.*, pp. 5-10.   ⁶*Ibid.*, pp. 40-41.

outlawing of idolatry among Tonghak members; (2) abstinence from eating fish and meat and from drinking and smoking; and (3) the use of one bowl of pure water in worship, because "water, having the qualities of purity, liquidity, and everpresence, is the origin of all natural things." The abstinence requirement was removed in the autumn of 1881 by the *Sinsa*, as a result of "word received from Heaven."[7]

In 1878, the Divine Teacher held the first regularly scheduled Tonghak worship service, implementing the *kaejŏp* (worship) principles previously promulgated by the founder. The *Kaejŏp* System consisted of: (1) deciding upon a fixed time for worship; (2) assembling believers at each locality during the scheduled worship period; and (3) studying the faith together. From this beginning, the Tonghak organization developed a system of church congregations similar to that of Christian denominations.[8]

In 1884, the *Sinsa*, recognizing the outstanding personality of Son Pyŏng-hi, brought him to Kayasa (a Buddhist temple), where Son prayed for forty-nine days. After this experience, and after the *Sinsa* had had a "vision," the latter dictated to Son the substance of the *Yungnim Chedo* (Six Responsibilities System) which had been revealed in the vision.[9] This system, which was subsequently followed throughout the Tonghak organization, provided that each local congregation *(p'o)*, and also the district and provincial headquarters, would have a staff composed of the following six types of officials who would exercise the specified responsibilities and who must possess the specified qualifications:

1. The *Kyojang,* or Chief Instructor, must possess honesty and a noble character.

2. The *Kyosu,* or teacher, must be a person of integrity and self-cultivation, with ability to spread the Tonghak doctrine.

3. The *Tojip,* or Chief Administrator, must be a person of persuasive, strong character, with a clear understanding of Tonghak principles and of the local situation.

4. The *Chipkang,* or Judge, is the man charged with maintaining Tonghak principles, and must be a person who can distinguish clearly between right and wrong.

5. The *Taejong,* or Counselor, should be a man of impartiality, industry, and generosity.

6. The *Chongjŏng,* or Censor, should be a frank-speaking person with a strong character.[10]

In 1887, four years after the institution of this system, the *Sinsa* ordered that Tonghak followers must first present their problems to the six responsible

---

[7]*Ibid.,* pp. 24, 30.   [8]*Ibid.,* pp. 25-26.   [9]*Ibid.,* p. 32.

[10]*Ibid.,* p. 34. See also Chōsen No Ruiji Shūkyō [Pseudo-Religions in Korea], Statistical Study No. 42, (Seoul: Japanese Government General in Korea, 1935), pp. 42-44.

officials in the local Tonghak unit before approaching the *Sinsa* himself. The purposes of this ruling were probably to strengthen the local organizations and to standardize administrative procedures, rather than to place the *Sinsa* beyond the reach of the rank and file. In August, 1889, the Divine Teacher temporarily suspended the Six Responsibilities System, to permit the local Tonghak officers to avoid pursuit by government officials.[11]

In the spring of 1886, the *Sinsa* predicted to his followers that there would be a serious epidemic and instructed them to take certain specific health measures. These health instructions appear remarkably advanced and constructive, having come from an uneducated, untraveled man living in the hinterlands of a backward country such as Korea in the 1880's. The instructions were: (1) do not mix old cooked rice with newly cooked rice; (2) reboil left-over food before eating it; (3) do not spit indiscriminately, and cover the sputum over with dirt from the roadside before going on; (4) after an elimination, cover the feces over with dirt; (5) be careful in disposing of dirty water; and (6) clean the interior of the house twice daily.

When the predicted epidemic actually materialized in July, 1886, no Tonghak members became afflicted, although many other Koreans were dying. This fact attracted attention and led many outsiders to join the Tonghak cult. One result of these developments was that, on January 24, 1887, the *Sinsa* issued an official order requiring all believers, including himself, to observe forty-nine days of regular prayer twice a year, in the spring and autumn, as an established part of the religious activities of devout Tonghak members.[12]

The Abortive Revolt of 1871

Pressure mounted among the members of the harassed Tonghak organization for forceful action to alleviate their suffering and to clear the name of their Great Divine Teacher who had been executed as a traitor. Ch'oe Si-hyŏng, the *Sinsa*, nevertheless generally succeeded in holding the organization to the founder's basic principles of loyalty to the King and noninvolvement in openly political activities. Before 1892, when events were rapidly leading to the outbreak of the Tonghak Rebellion of 1894, the one notable exception was an unsuccessful local revolt in 1871, carried out over the opposition of the *Sinsa* by a young Tonghak member named Yi P'il.

Yi P'il was a native of Mun'gyŏng, a town in Kyŏngsang Province, the area where both Ch'oe Si-hyŏng and Ch'oe Che-u (the *Taesinsa*) had lived and where the latter had established the Tonghak cult. Yi had been converted to the Tonghak doctrine by the *Taesinsa* himself in 1863 and had then engaged in spreading the doctrine. While hiding out in the Chiri Mountain area in southwestern Korea, he learned of the execution of the *Taesinsa* and vowed to redress this wrong. He held his vow in abeyance for some six years, because of the necessity of hiding out from the authorities and because he was unable to

---

[11]*Ch'ŏndogyo Ch'ang Kŏn Sa*, Pt. II, pp. 39-40.   [12]*Ibid.*, p. 38.

locate the *Sinsa* (Ch'oe Si-hyŏng) who was himself in hiding. In the year 1870, Yi P'il learned of the *Sinsa*'s whereabouts and sent him a message recounting his own experience as a Tonghak follower and asking the *Sinsa*'s advice and support in the planning and execution of an uprising designed to avenge the honor of the martyred *Taesinsa*. The *Sinsa*, not knowing Yi P'il and suspecting possible treachery, refused to receive the messenger. In the early spring of 1871, Yi renewed his efforts to contact the *Sinsa*, but his messenger was refused reception five times. Finally, the *Sinsa* himself went with the messenger to Yŏngwŏl where Yi P'il was living. Yi received the *Sinsa* with great respect and asked for his support in the plan to clear the name of the *Taesinsa*. The *Sinsa*'s attitude on armed rebellion is succinctly expressed in the following reply which he gave to Yi P'il:

> The intention to redress the wrong against our former teacher is right, as far as justice is concerned. We who are fellow disciples have this feeling in common. However, major undertakings require a proper time and fortune, and, in my opinion, that occasion has not yet arrived. The reason is that, since the execution of our former teacher, the faith of most of the followers has not yet developed roots and also the attitude of the people is not yet favorable toward our Way. At this time when there is no popular understanding, if we should take action thoughtlessly, it would be like planting seed out of season. Failure would be certain. If there should be any further failure at this time, it would be impossible to rebuild the strength of the Great Way. Therefore, I suggest that you keep these things in mind and wait until a later time.[13]

Yi P'il disregarded the *Sinsa*'s advice and hurried off to the town of Mun'gyŏng, his birthplace, and led an uprising there on April 29, 1871, the seventh anniversary of the death of the martyred founder. Yi mobilized 500 people, commissioned himself as General, and led the group against the municipal government of Mun'gyŏng. They captured the Chief Magistrate, questioned him, and beheaded him. They seized arms there. Yi P'il then reorganized his force and attacked the neighboring town of Sangju, but met defeat at the hands of a composite force raised by the local officials of the surrounding area. More than 100 of Yi's men were captured, but he himself escaped. In the early fall of 1871, Yi P'il, with the collaboration of one Chŏng Ki-hyŏn, organized a second armed force and attacked Mun'gyŏng a second time. In this action Yi was caught and beheaded, and the rebellion was completely crushed, as the *Sinsa* had predicted.[14]

Korea as a Pawn in International Politics

During the period of Ch'oe Si-hyŏng's leadership of the Tonghak sect, historic changes were taking place in Korea's international position. In the decade beginning in 1866, a number of Western expeditions had attempted unsuccessfully to establish commercial and/or diplomatic relations with Korea. In 1876, however, the strong and determined leaders of Meiji Japan forced the Korean

---

[13]*Ibid.*, pp. 12-13.

[14]*Ibid.*, pp. 11-14, for the entire Yi P'il affair.

monarchy to abandon its long-held policy of isolation and to agree to a treaty establishing diplomatic-commercial relations between the two countries and granting extraterritorial rights to Japan. A diplomatic-commercial treaty with Korea was secured by the United States in 1882, and similar treaties were concluded by the other Western powers within the next several years.[15]

The conclusion of the Japanese-Korean treaty, which specifically recognized the independence of Korea from the Chinese Empire, marked a break in the traditional "elder brother—younger brother" relationship of China and Korea. However, the Korean court had agreed to conclude the treaty only when advised to do so by Li Hung-chang, the Chinese Viceroy, who hoped by this means to avoid a Sino-Japanese clash. Li also counseled the Korean government to negotiate the United States—Korean treaty of 1882, and, on the latter occasion, the Viceroy declared that the Korean government had complete control of the foreign and domestic affairs of Korea.

Between 1882 and 1885, however, the Chinese government came to believe that non-Chinese foreign influence in Korea was becoming a serious threat to Chinese interests. Rather than simply reinstituting the loose suzerainty which it had traditionally exercised over Korea, China considered it necessary to assert unchallengeable control. The Chinese were given an opportunity to initiate this new, forceful policy in the summer of 1882, when the ruling faction of Queen Min called for Chinese forces to quell a revolt of disgruntled soldiers.[16]

The rioters were "old style" Korean troops whose livelihood was being threatened, under the Min regime, by the establishment of a modern army, trained by the Japanese and supported by a small but influential party of Western-oriented reformers. The soldiers, seeking protection from an oppressive and unscrupulous paymaster, appealed to the *Taewŏngun*, the Queen's arch rival, who was only too eager for an opportunity to regain power. The vindictive ex-Regent capitalized on the grievances of the troops to stir them up against the Mins and against the reform party and the Japanese. During a period of ten days before the Chinese forces were able to intervene and restore order, the *Taewŏngun* held absolute power and destroyed many of his enemies. The Queen herself narrowly escaped death, but the Chinese, after removing the *Taewŏngun* to China for a three-year "vacation," restored the Queen's party to power.

The Queen, who had given token support to reform measures and foreign treaties largely to discredit and displace the *Taewŏngun*, had always been

---

[15]Ko Kwŏn-sam, *Chōsen Seiji-shi Ko* [Outline of Korean Political History] (Tokyo: Nagada Shōten, 1933), pp. 132-133. See also William L. Langer (ed.), *An Encyclopedia of World History* (Boston: Houghton Mifflin, 1948), pp. 885-887; and Hulbert, *op. cit.*, pp. 215-245.

For text of US-Korean Treaty, see W. M. Malloy (ed.), *Treaties, Conventions, etc.* (Washington: Govt. Printing Office, 1910), Vol. I, pp. 334-339; for text of Japanese-Korean Treaty, see *British and Foreign State Papers*, Vol. LXVII, pp. 530-533.

[16]Clarence N. Weems, Jr., *op. cit.*, pp. 33-34. Dr. Weems cites T. F. Tsiang, "Sino-Japanese Diplomatic Relations, 1870-1894," *The Chinese Social and Political Science Review*, Vol. XVII (April, 1935), pp. 1-106; and T. C. Lin, "Li Hung-chang: His Korean Policies, 1870-1885," *Ibid.*, Vol. XIX (1935-36), pp. 203-233.

basically pro-Chinese. With the progressively increasing exercise of Chinese power in Korea after 1882, the Queen's faction became more and more inclined to follow conservative policies at the expense of the liberal program of the reformists.

The reform group, known as the Kaehwa Party, was led by Kim Ok-kyun and four other outstanding and patriotic young Koreans who looked to Japan as the most promising source of help in instituting modern reforms in Korea. These five leaders, over a period of several years, had trained themselves and some sixty other able young Koreans in Japan and had developed fairly constructive plans for governmental and social reform. In December, 1884, in a desperate attempt to accomplish this program before it was too late, the reform group gained control of the King's person in a quick and bloody coup.[17]

Scheduled Japanese military support did not arrive in time, and Chinese forces were able to recapture the King and put down the revolt. Japan intervened to gain redress for the loss of Japanese lives and property involved in the suppression of the coup. A war between China and Japan was averted at this time, however, by the conclusion of the Li-Ito Convention at Tientsin in April, 1885. This agreement provided that each power would evacuate its troops from Korea within four months and would notify the other power before dispatching troops there in the future. Chinese influence upon the Korean Government continued to be dominant and, beginning in the latter part of 1885, was exercised through the shrewd Resident, Yüan Shi-k'ai. The Japanese, however, were maintaining constant economic and political pressure and preparing themselves militarily for an eventual showdown.[18]

During the period 1885-1894, the principal Western powers interested in Korean developments were the United States, Great Britain, and Russia. France and Germany, actively involved in other parts of the Far East, maintained diplomatic representatives in Korea, but played minor diplomatic roles there. The United States' position toward Korea was:

> ... that while the United States sympathized with [Korea] and desired to see its sovereignty respected, we must maintain toward it and the other powers an attitude of impartial neutrality; that our influence could be exerted with Japan only in a friendly way, and that in no event could we intervene jointly with other powers.[19]

Great Britain supported China's claim to suzerainty over Korea, because a maintenance of the *status quo* in Korea appeared to Britain to offer the best prospects for preserving the delicate balance of power in the Far East and safeguarding British trade. The one power which Britain most feared might upset

---

[17]Clarence N. Weems, Jr., *op. cit.*, pp. 18-67.

[18]Ko Kwŏn-sam, *op. cit.*, pp. 134-141. For text of convention, see Harley Farnsworth MacNair, *Modern Chinese History Selected Readings* (Shanghai: The Commercial Press, Ltd., 1933), pp. 514-515.

[19]Mr. Gresham to Mr. Bayard, U. S. Dept. of State, *Foreign Relations of the United States*, 1894, App. I (Washington: Government Printing Office, 1895), No. 28, p. 37.

this balance was her perennial enemy, Russia. The rare shows of force by Britain respecting Korea during this period—notably the occupation of Port Hamilton off the southern Korean coast from May, 1885 to February, 1887— were made for the purpose of blocking Russian designs on Korea.[20] Russia likewise considered Great Britain her principal enemy in the Far East but, having unfulfilled ambitions of gaining a dominant position in Korea herself (the Trans-Siberian Railway was not yet completed), had no desire to see the dominance of China in Korea supplanted by that of an aggressive Japan. At the same time, distrust of Britain prevented Russia from joining the former in any effective action to prevent Sino-Japanese hostilities over Korea.[21] It was therefore in the interests of the United States, Great Britain, and Russia, for differing reasons, to prevent a showdown between China and Japan. However, since none of the powers was prepared to take forceful unilateral action and since there was insufficient community of interest to impel them to take effective action in concert, Japan was, in effect, given a free hand to apply her own solution to the problem of Korea.

The Tonghaks Petition the Government

The Korean government, having rid itself of all reformist influences, became increasingly venal and ruthless in its dealings with the Tonghaks. Despite this government policy, or because of it, Tonghak strength continued to grow. In 1892, the alarmed government authorities launched an intensified drive to wipe out the sect. Early in that year, Cho Pyŏng-sik, the King's Governor of Ch'ungch'ŏng Province, began the implementation of this policy of eradication by issuing an edict making the Tonghak sect illegal in his province. Ch'oe Si-hyŏng, the *Sinsa*, still did not consider that the time was ripe for strong action. Finally, however, in response to mounting pressure from his followers, he agreed to make formal representations to the government, with a view to clearing the name of the martyred *Taesinsa* and effecting the removal of the stamp of illegality from the Tonghak organization. He wrote a circular letter to his Tonghak groups, advocating formal petitioning of the government.[22] The *Sinsa* then prepared a petition which he dispatched both to Governor Cho of Ch'ungch'ŏng Province and to Governor Yi Kyŏng-sik of Chŏlla Province. The forcefulness of the petition was enhanced, with respect to Governor Yi of Chŏlla, by the fact that it was delivered to him from a mass meeting of several thousand Tonghak members which assembled at Samnye (near Chŏnju, the Chŏlla provincial capital) on December 19, 1892. The petition read:

[20]R. Stanley McCordock, *British Far Eastern Policy 1894-1900* (New York: Columbia Univ. Press, 1931), pp. 76-84. Also George N. (Lord) Curzon, *Problems of the Far East* (New York: Longmans, Green, 1896), pp. 206-217. See also Ko Kwŏn-sam, *op. cit.,* pp. 159-160.

[21]*Krasnyi Arkhiv,* Vol. L, p. 32, quoted in David J. Dallin, *The Rise of Russia in the Far East* (New Haven: Yale Univ. Press, 1949), p. 37; Abraham Yarmolinsky (Trans. and Ed.), *The Memoirs of Count Witte* (Garden City: Doubleday, Page, 1921), pp. 82-85; Curzon, *op., cit.,* pp. 209-213; McCordock, *op. cit.,* p. 80; Ko Kwŏn-sam, *op. cit.,* p. 160.

[22]*Ch'ŏndogyo Ch'ang Kŏn Sa,* Pt. II, pp. 45-46.

Our teacher, Ch'oe of Yongdam, receiving a direct order from God, tried to spread widely the virtue of Tonghak as the Way in which Heaven and Man are one, in order to save the people from suffering. Unfortunately, he was falsely accused of being a heretic and was martyred in Taegu. Ah, what a tragedy! We are well-trained disciples of Ch'oe, our Master. Therefore, the one object of redressing this wrong occupies our thoughts at all times: we dream of it when we are asleep; we swallow it when we eat; and even if we have one minute's rest, we think of it then. How, then, can this purpose be neglected? It might be possible for one to desceibe Po i and Shu ch'i as self-seeking persons, but the accusation that our teacher embraced the Western religion is so unjust that we vow not to cease our present action until this point has been clarified, even though we should be killed ten thousand times. . . . For thirty years, despite our bitterness, we have been patient and have not redressed the wrong or removed the cloud from the Great Way. Actually, this has been due to our lack of ability and integrity . . . Since the people at large do not understand our principles, they point us out as heretics on the basis of groundless rumors. Nowadays, however, there are numerous religions other than Confucianism, but the people, disregarding these other religions, repudiate and oppress only our Tonghak, calling our doctrine "Sŏhak." Our teacher was born in the East and studied in the East; how can East become West? Inasmuch as he learned the doctrine from God and Man, the punishment of our teacher does not seem right, because it amounts to condemnation of God. . . . The responsible officials in various localities, pointing us out as a faction of "Sŏhak," have relentlessly pursued us, arrested us, confiscated our property, and killed or wounded our people continually. Moreover, there are numerous places where our houses have been destroyed and our property confiscated by wealthy people of towns and villages who, learning of the government action elsewhere, took matters into their own hands. Almost all of the people who are known to be followers of the Way have been driven from their homes and have no place to settle down. . . . It is said that we are being suppressed because we are heretics, and that people who opposed Yang tzŭ and Mo tzŭ with words were called holy men. It may be all right to oppose with words, but I have never heard of anyone who opposed Yang tzŭ and Mo tzŭ by confiscating property and killing people being regarded as a holy man. . . . We, as ordinary subjects of His Majesty's benevolent reign, after having read the Confucian writings, living on His Majesty's soil, are determined to follow this new doctrine only because we want people to reform themselves, to be loyal to their King, to show filial piety to their parents, to respect their teachers, and to show friendship to their fellow men. We have no intention other than this. Therefore, the great desires for which we who follow the Way with wholehearted devotion are praying day and night are the welfare of the country, the security of the people, and the spreading of virtue throughout the land. . . . I specifically request Your Excellency to: (1) forward to His Majesty a recommendation that the wrong against our former teacher be redressed; and (2) issue orders to all the local authorities to save our remaining people from death.[23]

To this moderate and reasoned appeal, Governor Yi, after a delay of five days, replied brusquely, saying, in effect: "Tonghak has been outlawed. Why do you continue to practice this heresy and allow yourselves to be captives of this doctrine, and commit crimes?"[24] The following day, December 25, the Tonghak leaders appealed again to Governor Yi, expressing disappointment

---

[23]*Ibid.*, pp. 46-48. *Po i* and *Shu ch'i* were brothers renowned in Chinese legendary history as paragons of integrity and faithfulness; it would therefore be almost unthinkable to accuse them of being self-seeking. *Yang tzŭ* and *Mo tzŭ* were two Chinese philosophers who were considered unorthodox or even heretical by strict followers of Confucius. See William F. Mayers, *The Chinese Reader's Manual* (Shanghai: Kelly and Walsh, 1924), p. 181; pp. 162 and 284.

[24]*Ch'ŏndogyo Ch'ang Kŏn Sa*, Pt. II, p. 48.

at the fact that his reply, rather than showing any consideration for the Tong-hak grievances, simply reiterated the false accusations of which they had complained. They repeated their original plea for justice, and "tens of thousands" of them refused to leave the gate of the Governor's Residence until he gave a complete reply. Two days later, the Governor issued this order to his local officials:

> Since the Tonghak doctrine is outlawed by the Government, you will prohibit the practice of this doctrine in accordance with the law. However, I have heard that in many places the proscription [of Tonghak] has been used as a pretext for confiscating the property and injuring the lives of Tonghak people. How can such action be justified by the law? Immediately upon receipt of this message, you will: (1) search your jurisdiction for any Tonghak followers and persuade them to give up their beliefs and return to the righteous doctrine [Confucianism]; and (2) forbid any Government employees from confiscating even one penny's worth of property from anyone.[25]

The protesting Tonghaks broke up their meeting when this order was issued. They were not satisfied, since the Governor had not considered clearing the name of the martyred *Taesinsa*, but they were gratified that the Governor had sent out orders prohibiting confiscation of property. The Tonghak members therefore agreed to return to their homes and to pass the word among their fellow members to come out of their hiding places, return to their homes, and resume their occupations.[26]

Early in 1893, it became apparent that no actual change in conditions would result from the Tonghak appeals on the provincial level. Thereupon, a mass meeting of Tonghak members was held at Poŭn in Ch'ungch'ŏng Province to prepare a direct appeal to the King. Ch'oe Si-hyŏng, the *Sinsa*, approved this course of action and presided at the meeting. Methods to be followed in presenting the petition were considered in some detail. A particularly serious problem was that of selecting a chief signer, since it had frequently happened that this individual (the person whose name appeared first among the signers of a petition to the King) had been beheaded. The Tonghak leaders at Poŭn therefore asked for volunteers, and when about thirty responded to this call, one of them, Pak Kwang-ho, was selected as chief signer. Other signers included nine representatives of the Tonghak membership and three Principal Leaders: Son Pyŏng-hi, Kim Yŏn-guk, and Son Ch'ŏn-min. Son Ch'ŏn-min was designated to draft the petition and one Nam Hong-wŏn, a well known and highly skilled calligrapher, put it in final form. Sŏ Pyŏng-hak, one of the more militant Tonghak leaders, was sent as a delegate to Seoul, where he set up a Tonghak headquarters.[27]

The petition to the King was, in its substance, almost an exact repetition of the previous appeals to the provincial governors, asking redress of the wrong done to the late Great Divine Teacher. Like the earlier petitions, the appeal to the King contained no antiforeign sentiments. The most significant point

---

[25]*Ibid.*, pp. 48-49.   [26]*Ibid.*   [27]*Ibid.*, pp. 49-51.

about the text prepared for the King was that the Tonghak representatives went to great lengths to express in the humblest and most unequivocal terms their complete loyalty to the Throne. This attitude is particularly apparent in the introductory portion of the petition, which reads:

> We, *yuhak* [graduate Confucian scholars without official status] from each province, represented by Pak Kwang-ho, bowing deeply in profound respect and having humbly bathed ourselves, respectfully submit the following petition. Your majesty who from the beginning has ruled the world, who enjoys ever-increasing prosperity, who from the beginning has strengthened our ethical system and has been righteous, holy, brilliant, and faithful, who is equitable in recognizing merit and great virtue, is comparable to *Yao, Shun, Yü,* and *T'ang* [wise and benevolent rulers of China]. By order of Heaven, this nation was formed and Your Majesty became our divine King. When people are in need, they seek their parents, and when they suffer, they seek God. This is the law of Nature. Your Majesty is both God and parents to us, and we are your humble children. In a time of such suffering and need, we cannot but appeal to Your Majesty in unison even though we realize that this action will be offensive to Your Majesty.[28]

After the Tonghak petitioners and additional thousands of Tonghak members had reached Seoul, it developed that Sŏ Pyŏng-hak (the delegate commissioned to establish the Seoul headquarters) and another member named Sŏ In-ju were attempting to pursue a course of action contrary to that agreed upon at the Poŭn convention. These two men, disapproving the petitioning of the King and advocating more forceful action, disguised themselves and infiltrated into the government troops in Seoul, with a view to overthrowing the government and eliminating the corrupt officials. This activity became known to the Seoul police chief, who ordered a thorough investigation of all the hotels where Tonghak members were staying. This alerted the *Sinsa,* who decided that immediate action was imperative, even though this course would make it impossible to route the petition through the regular channel (the *Chŏng Wŏn,* or Royal Board of Registry). According to the Ch'ŏndogyo account, he then ordered all Tonghak followers in Seoul to gather at the gate of the King's palace, and "many tens of thousands" of them knelt in front of the gate and wailed in unison so that the sound "shook the city and echoed from the neighboring mountains." This account goes on to state that, after the representatives had maintained their position before the gate for some two days and nights (March 29-31), a royal messenger issued an oral order to the petitioners, in the name of the King, to take their petition through the proper channel. While the Tonghak leaders were attempting to make these arrangements, the King himself, hearing the continued wails of the Tonghak representatives, sent out his personal messenger with an order to the Tonghaks to go home and return to their occupations. The oral order was accompanied by an oral promise that, if the Tonghaks obeyed, the King would "carry out their wishes." Upon receipt of the instructions and promise of the King, the *Sinsa* ordered his followers to obey, and the demonstration ended.[29]

---

[28]*Ibid.,* p. 51.   [29]*Ibid.,* pp. 53-54.

On the following day (April 1), a formal decree appeared in the official Gazette, "in which His Majesty admonished the Tonghak, in a fatherly way, to abandon their false doctrines and study the true Confucian wisdom. If they did not heed his admonitions he would be compelled to chastise them even unto death."[30] This official document apparently included no royal promise of improved treatment of the Tonghaks in return for obedience.

The official American account of the petitioning of the King by the Tonghak representatives essentially supports the Tonghak version, but gives a much more meaningful account of the number of people directly and indirectly involved:

> The strength of the organization, or the strength of its backing in Seoul, may be inferred from the fact that not long ago to be suspected of having affiliations with the Tong Hak was to insure persecution and death; and to-day they declare themselves boldly at the gate of the palace asking, almost demanding, recognition. Only forty appeared there, but it is supposed there are many hundreds, perhaps thousands, in the city, and these forty were renewed from time to time as they became fatigued. The birthday of the crown prince occurred on the 24th of March, and the quagas [Kwagŏ] or examinations that were held in honor of the event have been the pretext under which great numbers from the country have entered the city, a certain proportion of them, no doubt, belonging to this sect.[31]

Signs of Antiforeignism

The American Minister did not know the content of the Tonghak petition to the King. Depending primarily on information from government officials who apparently desired to create sufficient uneasiness among foreign representatives to assure themselves of foreign military protection, the Minister stated that the petition "is supposed to contain a protest against foreigners and Christianity, with the request that His Majesty should intervene."[32] As previously noted, this suspicion of antiforeignism is not supported by the content of the official Tonghak petitions or of Tonghak doctrine itself. However the American Minister and other foreign representatives were, in fact, given good cause for concern by certain strongly antiforeign actions taken more or less concurrently with the official Tonghak effort to memorialize the throne, and apparently instigated by persons in some way associated with the Tonghak movement. The American Minister, Mr. Heard, gave to the Secretary of State a careful and reasoned analysis of the dangerous potentialities of this aspect of the movement, as distinguished from the Tonghak sect itself and the sincere, constructive doctrine of Ch'oe Che-u:

> To these principles no objection can be made; but to the sincere believers must be added many who believe in the success of the movement and who wish to be on the winning side; and by many (it is reported) who are hostile to the Roman Catholics. These

---

[30]Mr. Heard to Mr. Gresham, U.S. Dept. of State, *Foreign Relations of the United States*, 1894, App. 1 (Washington: Government Printing Office, 1895), No. 1, p. 7.

[31]*Ibid.*, p. 6.   [32]*Ibid.*

are thought, either rightly or wrongly, to be protected by the priests from the exactions of the magistrates, to which all others are liable; and if there is anything to call forth hostility from the mandarin it is to see what he considers as his lawful prey withdrawn from his clutches; and all those who must pay hate without measure those who are exempt. Many, it is said, of bad character, enroll themselves under the priests to escape the payment of their just debts. I am now only repeating remarks which are not unusual among Koreans, in which, no doubt, there is much exaggeration.

So much for the sect as a sect proper. But we must also look upon it as an organized body, which may be used by a political party for political purposes; and there are many who regard the present movement as only a demonstration of political intrigue.

What the Government fears, if it fears anything, is not so much what may take place in Seoul, where they have a body of disciplined troops who are probably free from the contamination, as of an outbreak in the southern provinces, where there is a certain feeling against foreigners, or against Catholics, and where alone apparently it exists. It was in Kiong-sang Do [Kyŏngsang Province] that the attacks were made on Pere Robert near Tai-ku [Taegu], and recently on another priest at Kam-san. Ch'ung-ch'ong Do, Kiong-sang Do, and Cholla Do are said to be full of these people, and it is impossible to say how far their tenets may have gained over the officials.[33]

Mr. Heard's account continues, with particular emphasis upon the mysterious appearance, on the property of the American Protestant (Presbyterian and Methodist) missions, of two bitterly anti-Christian and antiforeign placards which, though anonymous, contained language tending to identify the author with the Tonghak movement. The first placard, apparently addressed primarily to native converts to Christianity, was posted on the night of March 31 just after the Tonghak petitioners had been dispersed from the palace gate. This notice was worded, in translation, as follows:

Alas, alas! my little children, receive the words of this notice with reverential fear.

Surely our Eastern land has been a Kingdom of propriety and rectitude for several thousand years. The growth of this Kingdom of propriety and rectitude, and the practice thereof, even this, have hardly been achieved; how much less that of other creeds?

An inspection of the books of these creeds, and an examination of the doctrines they inculcate, disclose the fact that, in their so-called teaching, what is styled reverence of heaven is really rebellion against heaven; what is called love toward mankind is a delusive mockery and a stealing of men's hearts.

Heaven and hell! what talk is this? Although our people talk of spirits and genii, who ever saw one? Although these people talk about heaven, who ever saw heaven?

But upon you, you fools and foolish strangers, who delude and bewilder with empty nothings; who believe in chaotic incoherence; who forsake sound and great principles and follow after "universal love"; who cast aside ancestral sacrifice and practice these extravagant teachings. This is what the sages and worthies meant when they said "without father," "without sovereign."

In ancient days the illustrious ministers and advisers of our glorious and sacred rulers founded seminaries and established schools of thought for the gradual development of the principles of charity and patriotism, and the covering, as it were, with a cloak of civilization the regions of the east and west. There was universal good government brought about. Now, strange doctrines are spread abroad like a network; delusion and falsehood have sprung up like weeds. Thus is misrule and disorder universally prevalent.

---

[33] *Ibid.,* pp. 6-7.

You are the descendants of these able ministers and advisers, and you bring dishonor upon your illustrious ancestry. Is it not pitiful? Is it not a detestable state of things?

The greatness of our doctrines proceeds from heavenly brightness — heavenly effulgence. Dare you, then, plunge from these into profligacy and bring shame and dishonor on this teaching?

The principles of universal good government are to be found in the proximity of our ruler who dwells in the midst of perfect refinement. Can you but be afraid of what you are doing? Can you but beware?

Alas, alas! my little children; follow the great doctrine; make men of your men; burn these books. So shall you live in an infinitesimal degree as you ought to live.

(Here follow four lines of unintelligible verse.)

An anonymous notice issued by Mr. Kung-i, of Pai-ling Shan, betwixt night and day in the second moon of the cyclical year Kuei ssu (1893).[34]

The second placard forwarded by Mr. Heard was discovered on the gate of a mission compound on April 4. This outburst, if not "much more scurrilous than the other," as the Minister described it, was certainly more threatening, and more specifically and intensely antiforeign in tone and content. In translation, it read:

To the head of the religion addressed:

You, crowd, listen with your ears. Fortune is decreasing and the doctrine of the world is being lost. The Royal Ancestral Temple has been befouled by interrelation with barbarians. There is no promise in the treaties permitting the establishment of schools and the propagation of religion.

You, heads of religions, have one by one come in saying, "We come to worship God," which you do by prayer only; you say you believe in Jesus, but show it only by hymns. Among you there is neither sincerity nor sense; you never perform what you preach. You say, "Honor thy parents," yet during their life you neither care for nor obey them, and after their death (you have) neither tears nor (funeral) ceremony. Is this human nature? When you marry you first mate (like beasts), and without shame even enter upon marriage a second time. Upon the least evidence of incompatibility you break the marriage tie. Your crowd, originally beggars, sold themselves for the wages offered by the church. Your hearts are full of covetousness for good houses and an easy life.

At first you deceived the children of (native) aristocrats by promises of instruction in English and Chinese, but finally you force them into your religion, and out of the money intended for scholars' food and clothing you have to get your squeeze. Is not that vile? You know that your trips for preaching are only pretexts for sight-seeing and the sale of books. You call this preaching! If there is an eternal hell, you shall first enter it. Do you not fear this? Why, then, discuss with you? We religious scholars, how could we hold converse with a miserly crowd? To speak clearly: You crowd, gather together your possessions and depart quickly. If you don't, with the armor and shields of patriots, and crying out your sins, we will come and attack you on the 7th of the third moon.

Know the same.[35]

On April 20, 1893, the American Minister reported to the Secretary of State that, although no serious incident had yet occurred, "one can hardly help

---

[34]*Ibid.*, pp. 8-9. The use of Chinese romanizations for the personal name, the place name, and the cyclical year designation in the final note suggests that the translation was done by a non-Korean who probably did not have firsthand knowledge of the Tonghak movement.

[35]*Ibid.*, p. 9. The 7th day of the third moon was April 22, 1893.

feeling that something serious is preparing. . . ."[36] The cause for concern was genuine. A few days before, members of the Tonghak organization had posted, on the palace gate of the Governor of Chŏlla Province, a signed declaration which contained a brief, superficial version of certain ethical principles included in the Tonghak doctrine. The statement consisted in the main, however, of a revolutionary battle cry aimed specifically at the expulsion of "Japanese and foreign rebels and thieves."[37] The complete text of this manifesto, as forwarded in translation by the American Minister, was as follows:

Men have three tasks which confront them in the fulfillment of the duties of life.

(1) The task of laying down rules or limitations of conduct under which they shall carry out the requirements of loyalty to their fullest extent and, if needs be, to sacrifice their lives as servants of their country.

(2) To put forth all their efforts in the direction of loyalty and filial piety and to die, if needs be, for the sake of their personal belongings.

(3) To maintain widowed chastity and to die, if needs be, in the fulfillment of conjugal obligations.

Life and death are the appointed lot of all mankind; this is the unfailing law, whatever may betide. Those who are born in times of freedom from trouble and in periods of peace and happiness should pursue the path of patriotism and filial piety with a joyous heart, while, on the other hand, those who live in seasons of danger and difficulty should sacrifice their lives in the cause of patriotism and of filial piety. This is the task of all true servants of the state, and is a task that may devolve upon them in the course of the permutations of things. Those who love their lives are opposed by the difficulty of sacrificing their lives in the service of their King and their parents. Those who are ready to sacrifice their lives will willingly accept the task of giving them up for their King or their parents, and no one who clings to life can be a true subject or son. Those who are ready to part joyfully with life are the men who are capable of building principles of loyalty and filial piety upon a sure foundation.

Japanese and foreign rebels and thieves are now introduced into the very bowels of our land and anarchy has reached its zenith. Just look round on the capital under present conditions. It is the lair and den of barbarians. Think of the oath of (the year) Yen Ch'en,[a] of the disgrace of (the year) Ping-tzu![b] Can you bear to forget it? Can you bear to talk of it? Our three thousand millions of people in the Eastern Kingdom are now all in the grasp of wild beasts, and our ancestral homes of five thousand years' duration will shortly witness the disaster of dispersion and dismemberment. Alas for charity, patriotism, prosperity, prudence, filial piety, brotherly love, loyalty, and good faith! What has become of them all at the present time?

Let it, moreover, be remembered that most of the Japanese rebels cherish feelings of hatred toward us, and nurture within them the germs of disaster for our land which they will bring forth to our hurt. The danger threatens us at any moment, and can we regard the situation with tranquility? It might truly be said of the present condition of affairs that it is in proximity of brushwood.

We who issue this notice are simple, ignorant people, but for all that we are inheritors of the laws laid down by previous rulers, and we till the ground of our King to maintain our fathers and mothers. Although officials and people differ as honorables and commons,

---

[36]Mr. Heard to Mr. Gresham, *ibid.*, No. 4, p. 11.

[37]*Ibid.*, p. 13.

We desire to display our humble loyalty to the State and to secure to her loyal and upright servants their state emoluments to which they are entitled; but we are perplexed as to what to do, and it is not for us to institute comparisons as to the sincerity of our love for the King and loyalty to our country. There is an old saying, "When a great house is about to fall one piece of wood will not support it; when a great wave is about to roll in a single net will not keep it back."

We who number several millions, have sworn to the death that we will unite in one common effort to sweep out the Japanese and foreigners and bring them to ruin in our sage desire to render to our country the fidelity which even a dog will show to his master, and we humbly hope that everyone, within one common resolution, will combine their efforts and will select loyal and patriotic gentry to assist them in supporting the wish of the country. This is the earnest prayer of millions of people.

(Transcribed by the Tong-Hak men.)

a The year 1592, the date of the Japanese invasion.

b The year 1876, the date of the treaty of Kanghua with Japan.[38]

The American Minister succinctly evaluated the Tonghak developments of the early part of 1893 in the closing paragraph of a dispatch to the Secretary of State on May 16, 1893:

The Tonghak in themselves, I believe, are not dangerous. They seem to be quiet and peaceful, and would be content with little besides the rehabilitation of their founder and permission to practice their tenets; but they have no doubt collected to themselves hordes of discontented and poverty-stricken people. The whole may be, and probably is, under the control of a political party, bent on making trouble for the Government, but who this party is, and what its strength, we have as yet no knowledge.[39]

It is probable that the "party" referred to by the American Minister was actually the revolutionary element, composed partly of established Tonghak members and partly of opportunistic newcomers, which had been gaining influence in the Tonghak organization for some time and which became increasingly dominant after the abortive effort of the Tonghak representatives to memorialize the King. As previously noted, Sŏ In-ju and Sŏ Pyŏng-hak, two Tonghak leaders who opposed the petitioning of the King and who advocated revolutionary tactics, were present in Seoul at the time of the petitioning effort; they may well have been responsible for the antiforeign agitation on that occasion, as exemplified by the belligerent, anti-Christian and antiforeign declarations reported by the American Minister. As shall be seen, this revolutionary element soon came under the control of Chŏn Pong-jun, the principal leader of the Tonghak Rebellion.

The Inevitable Split

On April 25, 1893, when almost a month had passed since the Tonghak petitioners had returned to their homes in obedience to the King's order, a group of prominent regular leaders of the Tonghak sect met in the home of one of

---

[38]*Ibid.* In the same dispatch, Mr. Heard inclosed a translation of a blunt, anti-Japanese notice which had been posted on the gate of the Japanese Consulate in Seoul (apparently by Tonghak adherents), demanding immediate departure of the Japanese from Korea.

[39]Mr. Heard to Mr. Gresham, *Ibid.*, No. 6, p. 16.

their number in Kyŏngsang Province, in commemoration of the martyrdom of the founder, Ch'oe Che-u. These leaders included Son Pyŏng-hi and others who had participated in the petitioning of the King. They reported to Ch'oe Si-hyŏng, the *Sinsa*, who was also present for the occasion, that no new instructions had been received by the provincial officials from the King as a consequence of His Majesty's word to the Tonghak petitioners in Seoul. In fact, they said, the officials had become more oppressive than ever, with the result that the lives and property of Tonghak members were constantly in jeopardy. The *Sinsa*, when asked for his advice, ordered that a general meeting of Tonghak representatives be convened at Poŭn.[40]

The convention assembled immediately at Poŭn. When the *Sinsa* arrived he found "many tens of thousands" of his followers there. He established a headquarters and appointed leaders for the meeting by provinces, as each province had its own organization of delegates and its own banner. The official Ch'ŏndogyo account notes that the meeting was markedly quiet, dignified, and orderly, and that the manners and general behavior of the Tonghak representatives were so exemplary that the saying developed among the generally anti-Tonghak people in and around Poŭn that "although they follow Tonghak, their conduct is right."[41]

This Poŭn convention of April, 1893 discussed making a second petition to the King. Meanwhile, a rumor had reached the King to the effect that the Tonghaks, meeting in Poŭn, were organizing and training armed forces for a rebellion. The government discussed this report and considered issuing orders to General Hong Kye-hun, Commander in chief of government forces in the area, to bring the "rebellion" under control. However, a wise and respected cabinet minister, O Yun-jung, counseled the King that the truth of the rumor should be investigated before troops were sent. Thereupon, O, on the King's orders, went to Poŭn to determine the facts and returned with the report that the Tonghaks had no intention but to redress the wrong against their former teacher (Ch'oe Che-u), and that they had no weapons of any kind. The government then decided to send O Yun-jung back to Poŭn as the King's official representative, with broad authority to negotiate with the Tonghak leaders with a view to persuading them to dissolve their meeting. General Hong was ordered to station five hundred troops in Poŭn to enhance the effectiveness of O Yun-jung's efforts. On May 17, 1893, O, accompanied by the *Kunsu* (County Chief Magistrate) of Poŭn County, went to Poŭn and, in the name of the King, made an official pronouncement to the Tonghak members. He promised that the government would punish the corrupt officials who were oppressing Tonghak, and ordered the Tonghak people to return home and go back to work. The King's representative added that, upon compliance with this order, he would report this fact to the King, and "your desires will be fulfilled." The obvious

---

[40] *Ch'ŏndogyo Ch'ang Kŏn Sa*, Pt. II, pp. 53-54. [41] *Ibid.*, p. 56.

implication was that, if the order were not obeyed, the government would use force to bring compliance.

The convention was then disbanded by order of the *Sinsa,* despite the fact that the government's terms, like earlier overtures by the government, contained no specific commitment to remove the cloud of disgrace from the founder's name or to permit free practice of the Tonghak doctrine. The Tonghak element advocating direct, forceful action, urged upon the *Sinsa* the importance of clearing the name of the *Taesinsa* (Ch'oe Che-u) by attacking the government and forcefully reforming the nation. The *Sinsa* refused to authorize this course, and pled fervently with the dissenting group not to participate in such action. The *Sinsa,* still opposed in principle to the use of violent means in opposing the government, also was unwilling to risk destruction of the Tonghak movement by defying the political and military power of the government as represented by the King's special envoy and the commanding general in the area.[42]

The Accomplishments of Ch'oe Si-hyŏng

Ch'oe Si-hyŏng, the *Sinsa,* lacked the Master's magnetism and erudition, but possessed unusual skill in administration, in standardizing Tonghak ritual and religious observances, and in giving practical application to doctrinal principles laid down by the revered founder, Ch'oe Che-u. Both principle and expediency dictated that the *Sinsa* should place major emphasis on passive reform techniques in organizing and developing the Tonghak movement. This approach was integral to the fundamental Tonghak concept that sincere adherence to Tonghak (Ch'ŏndogyo) principles would provide spiritual relief from oppression and that application of these principles to Korean society and government would result ultimately in fundamental social, economic, and political changes beneficial to the whole nation. In short, since the desired changes would eventually take place through evolutionary processes as long as the faithful worked sincerely toward those ends, revolutionary techniques were both unnecessary and inconsistent with the doctrine. Moreover, normal prudence and experience justified the position taken by the *Sinsa* that direct action (even peaceful, formal representations to the government), taken prematurely, would result in swift and damaging countermeasures against the proscribed Tonghak cult, and possibly in the extinction of the movement.

The principal passive reform techniques employed by the Tonghak movement under Ch'oe Si-hyŏng's leadership may be grouped and evaluated as follows:

The Development of a Nucleus of Devoted, Indoctrinated Followers

The development of such a nucleus would have been impossible had it not been for the genius of Ch'oe Che-u in conceiving and articulating a doctrine or ideology which appealed to certain fundamental drives of a significant seg-

---

[42]*Ibid.,* pp. 54-56; Kang Chae-ŏn, *op. cit.,* No. II, Nov. 1954, p. 19.

ment of the Korean people. As has been seen, Ch'oe's doctrine filled a vacuum in the spiritual life of nineteenth century Koreans, appealing both to the intellect and to the Korean predilection for the mystical or superstitious. Moreover, the content of the doctrine was such as to furnish the basis for a dynamic social-economic-political program to motivate and activate a nucleus of followers. It was the magnetic personality of Ch'oe Che-u himself that instilled in his followers a personal devotion to him and to his ideas. His martyrdom magnified this spirit of devotion and created a new sense of unity based upon a common determination to clear the name of the Great Divine Teacher. The development of this faithful nucleus was perfected by Ch'oe Si-hyŏng, the *Sinsa*. He implemented the founder's ideals of personal righteousness and social reform by laying down specific codes of personal conduct and specific social standards, with reference to actual contemporary conditions. Perhaps more importantly, he reduced to more concrete terms the ritual and other religious forms of the cult. Such forms as (1) praying for forty-nine days at regular periods, (2) giving thanks to God when preparing food, and (3) using clean water, both for cooking and as a symbol in worship, were distinguishing marks of the devout and encouraged the growth of an *esprit de corps* among faithful Tonghak members.

The rapid spread of the Tonghak doctrine and of the movement inspired by it was entirely the work of this devoted, disciplined band of disciples. The utilization of this personal approach was consistent with the nature of the doctrine, and therefore would probably have been favored by the Tonghak leaders even under very different political conditions. But the strong emphasis on this means of spreading the movement was dictated primarily by the consistently hostile political climate of the period. The Tonghak movement found itself not only deprived of any governmental or other officially approved agency through which to operate, but also officially outlawed and suppressed. Despite these difficulties, the devoted Tonghak disciples, both by precept and by example, were able to make a perceptible impression upon the thoughts and actions of the general population in the southern half of Korea. They also exerted at least indirect influence in some of the northern provinces.

The Establishment of Effective, Decentralized Administrative Controls

There was an over-all unity in the Tonghak movement. Despite the necessity to operate largely underground, the *Sinsa* was able to maintain virtually continuous contact with, and control over, all parts of the organizational structure, through the *toju* (Provincial Leaders) and *tojŏpchu* (District or County Leaders). Major emphasis, however, appears to have been placed upon the importance of having strong, dynamic, effectively controlled local groups or *p'o*. Although the *p'o* leaders *(chŏpchu)* were centrally appointed, they were selected on the basis of the qualities of leadership which they showed in their own groups. Each *p'o* also had its own administrative staff organized according to the Six Responsibilities System, and these local officials were empowered by the *Sinsa* to handle virtually all doctrinal and administrative problems for local members. The strength and cohesion of the *p'o* were further enhanced by the institution of the *Kaejŏp* (Worship) System, which provided for regularly scheduled worship services in each *p'o*. Perhaps the most powerful instrument of local autonomy was the Sŏngmi (Sincerity Rice) System, whereby each *p'o* supported itself and contributed to the support of higher Tonghak headquarters with rice, produced locally and collected from all faithful members at the rate of a spoonful per day. Though local autonomy was consistent with Tonghak religious and social principles, it was also a practical necessity, because of the unremitting persecution of the Tonghak sect. The local leaders needed authority to take emergency measures to protect their own groups when lack of time and of safe communications made constant central direction of the organization impossible.

The passive reform techniques employed by the Tonghak leaders were significantly successful among the rank and file of the Korean people. One important measure of this success was the progressive intensification of government suppression measures. The passive reform program would, of course, have been much more successful if the leaders had been able to utilize these and perhaps other passive techniques to convert or otherwise enlist the support of: (1) the small but potentially effective group of Western-oriented reformers at the seat of government in Seoul; and (2) strategically placed local or central government officials. It may be that the very features of Tonghak doctrine and method that appealed to the suppressed segments of the Korean population made it impossible for the movement to attract a broadly based, nation-wide following.

Petitioning the Government

The petitioning of the provincial and central authorities of the Korean Government by the Tonghak leaders was not an original Tonghak technique. In fact, this action is significant primarily because it was a traditional act, entered into by loyal subjects of the King who were thoroughly versed in, and devoted to, the established Confucian principles governing relations between the rulers and the ruled. This fact gave to the Tonghak petitions, and particularly to the petition to the King in the spring of 1893, a potential psychological value. One reason that this potential did not become a reality may have been the lack of well-organized and rapid media of public opinion. Undoubtedly the principal reason for this failure, however, was that at the time of the petitioning of the King a bitterly antiforeign tone became associated with the Tonghak movement. The first antiforeign placard did not appear until *after* the Tonghak petitioners had been turned away from the palace gate, and there is no proof that the placards were prepared with the knowledge or consent of the regular Tonghak leadership. These factors, however, did not prevent the development of a strong anti-Tonghak feeling among Western observers and among some Korean elements which had previously been indifferent to the movement. The only actual result of the futile petitioning efforts was that a substantial segment of the Tonghak membership became convinced that more forceful measures would be necessary if the movement was to gain redress for its grievances.

CHAPTER IV
THE TONGHAK REBELLION

With the refusal of Ch'oe Si-hyŏng to authorize the employment of forceful measures against the government in the spring of 1893, the long-nascent schism in the Tonghak movement became a reality. Ch'oe, the *Sinsa,* retained effective control of the large area known as Pukchŏp (literally "Northern Jurisdiction") which included all Tonghak organizations in the southeastern provinces of Kyŏnsang and Kangwŏn, as well as in the northern part of Ch'ungch'ŏng Province and in the northwestern provinces of Hwanghae and P'yŏngan. The area known as Namjŏp (Southern Jurisdiction), comprising the southwestern province of Chŏlla and the southern part of Ch'ungch'ŏng Province, came under the control of Chŏn Pong-jun, the able and controversial leader of the Tonghak Rebellion.[1]

The Rise of Chŏn Pong-jun as a Rebel Leader

Chŏn Pong-jun was born in 1854 in Kobu County, in the northern part of Chŏlla Province. He was from a prominent family whose members had traditionally been local bureaucrats. That is, they were members neither of the official class nor of the socially unaccepted lower classes. His father had chafed under the unjust and venal administrations of local officials, and had been executed for complicity in an uprising against a corrupt *kunsu* (county chief magistrate). Chŏn was therefore motivated by a desire to inflict vengeance upon the government.[2]

Although he came to be a well-to-do farmer, Chŏn was brought up in poverty. He had access to the Confucian Classics, however, and managed to acquire a good classical education. His enthusiasm for learning was demonstrated by his interest in teaching his fellows and also by his efforts to expand his knowledge through the study of traditional military tactics and through seeking historical information from the village elders.[3]

In the course of his studies, he acquired a thorough mastery of *Ch'amwisŏl* [The Theory of Interpretation of Omens]. (See Chapter II, above). According

---

[1] Kim Sang-gi, *op. cit.,* p. 120.

[2] *Ibid.,* pp. 77 ff.; Kang Chae-ŏn, *op. cit.,* No. 11, Nov. 1954, p. 14-15. Also see *Chōsen Jimmei Jisho* [Korean Biographical Dictionary] (Seoul: Japanese Govt. Gen. in Korea, 1927), p. 1988.

[3] Kim Sang-gi, *op. cit.,* p. 78; Kang Chae-ŏn, *op. cit.,* No. 11, Nov. 1954, pp. 14-15.

to this theory, as applied to rulers, good rule brought blessings from Heaven and bad rule brought natural catastrophe. Specifically, it had been predicted some years previously, on the basis of *Ch'amwisŏl*, that the Yi Dynasty of Korea would fall after it had been in power for five hundred years, that is, after 1892. Chŏn apparently came to believe these prophecies and to feel that he himself was the man destined to bring them to realization.[4]

Chŏn Pong-jun had become a Tonghak member at the age of 30, some nine years before his assumption of control of the militant wing of the Tonghak movement at the Poŭn Convention in 1893. He had studied the doctrine under the *Sinsa*, and had become a *chŏpchu* (leader of a local unit, or *p'o*) in his home district of Kobu, in Chŏlla Province. His experience in leading the farming people in their difficulties with the local authorities enabled him to link many of these people to the Tonghak movement and to enhance his prominence as a Tonghak leader.[5]

An evaluation of Chŏn Pong-jun's character and his motivations in leading the Tonghak Rebellion is presented at the end of this chapter. Probably the most important immediate motivating factor, however, was the extreme malfeasance of the *kunsu* (county chief magistrate) of Kobu County. Three specific acts of this *kunsu* during 1893 were: (1) taking advantage of the collapse of a river bridge to impress several hundred thousand people as slave laborers; (2) imposing on the farmers a water tax amounting to about 20 per cent of the rice crop and appropriating the receipts himself; and (3) levying forced contributions of rice upon tenant farmers under the pretense of charity for poor Buddhist monks and with the force of authority of the central government. Early in 1894, Chŏn led the local people in protesting these outrages. The *kunsu* ignored the protests, and when the Provincial Governor was appealed to, he reacted by rejecting the complaints and jailing the protestors.[6]

The First Stage of the Rebellion

The rejection by the Provincial Governor of the protests of the people of Kobu County was, in effect, a signal to Chŏn Pong-jun to launch the rebellion which he and his principal lieutenants (Kim Kae-nam and Son Hwa-jung) had been planning for some months. In accordance with these plans, Chŏn began the rebellion on February 19, 1894, by capturing Kobu County. With this base secured, Kim Kae-nam and Son Hwa-jung then moved to expand the base of operations, and by February 22 had established rebel control over the surrounding counties of Mujang, T'aein, and Puan. In each of these engagements, Chŏn's forces acquired government arms and food supplies. Thus, in a period

---

[4]Kim Sang-gi, *op. cit.*, pp. 77 ff. For the prediction of the fall of the dynasty, see also Mr. Heard to Mr. Gresham, *Foreign Relations*, 1894, App. I, No. 1, p. 7.

[5]Kim Sang-gi, *op. cit.*, pp. 77ff.; Kang Chae-ŏn, *op. cit.*, No. 11, Nov. 1954, pp. 14-15; *Ch'ŏndogyo Ch'ang Kŏn SA*, Pt. II. p. 57.

[6]Kim Sang-gi, *op. cit.*, pp. 77-80. Monks were used to collect the rice levy, and the bags bore the government seal.

of a few days, the untrained and crudely armed rebels, by means of quick, bold strokes against half-hearted resistance by government forces, had acquired a substantial base for future operations, as well as a considerable supply of arms and equipment for conducting such operations. For about three months, Chŏn and his subordinates consolidated their control over the captured area in Chŏlla Province and prepared for future battles against the government.

Chŏn built up support among the residents of the base area by two important measures which immediately dramatized the change of administration. First, he abolished the hated water tax, by which the government officials had milked the farmers of large proportions of their rice crops. Secondly, he distributed rice from the captured government stores.

Chŏn then conducted an extensive propaganda-recruitment campaign. He distributed throughout the country, by word of mouth and handbills, statements which expressed loyalty to the King and which described the purposes of the Rebellion as: (1) destruction of the *yangban* class (nobility), the center of official corruption; and (2) reestablishment of peace for the country and safety for the people. This statement of purposes contained no reference to clearing the founder's name and no specific reference to eliminating foreign influences; the latter point, however, is implied in "reestablishment of peace for the country."

In order to strengthen his manpower position and to have machinery to mobilize new people (both Tonghak believers and nonbelievers) along the route of march toward Seoul, Chŏn utilized the Tonghak organizational structure where it existed, and organized new local units *(p'o)* where expedient. All *p'o* under control of Chŏn Pong-jun's rebel administration were reorganized as local military control units, under a new system of military government. This was a distinct change from the orthodox Six Responsibilities System of administration which, under the direction of Ch'oe Si-hyŏng and Son Pyŏng-hi, had been designed to build up and administer each *p'o* as a strong group of believers in the Tonghak doctrine.[7]

Chŏn trained his swelling guerrilla forces for the northward march, using guns and horses commandeered from the local population. There appears to have been no change in battle tactics from those used in the initial quick offensives. Before the spring campaign began, Chŏn laid down for his military forces the following three principles of conduct:

1. Although you are obliged to fight, try to avoid injury to life.
2. Do not molest the lives of people in places on the route of march.
3. Do not station your forces nearer than three miles to a town where there is a person distinguished for his faithfulness to parents and King.[8]

For the civil administration of areas occupied by his forces, Chŏn Pong-jun issued the following twelve-point code:

---

[7]*Ibid.,* pp. 84 ff.   [8]*Ibid.,* p. 88.

1. The antagonism existing between Tonghak members and the government shall be wiped out, and mutual cooperation shall be sought.
2. Severe punishment shall be dealt out to greedy, corrupt officials.
3. High-handed, wealthy people shall be punished.
4. Unprincipled Confucian scholars and *yangban* shall be reprimanded and reformed.
5. All slave records must be burned.
6. The treatment of the *Ch'il Ch'ŏn* [Seven Lowest Official Occupations] shall be revised, and discriminatory headgear abolished.
7. Young widows shall be allowed to remarry.
8. All unnecessary taxation shall be entirely discontinued.
9. Employment of government officials shall be based on ability rather than family background.
10. Those who engage in conspiracy shall be severely punished.
11. All debts, public or private, incurred in the past shall be canceled.
12. Farm land shall be equitably redistributed.[9]

Although this code contains many constructive principles, it also includes a number of instructions which encouraged acts of intimidation and violence on the part of Chŏn's forces. The actual performance of Chŏn's civil administrators appears to have incorporated some of the very practices against which the rebellion had ostensibly been aimed. The following account by a contemporary American observer, though not specifically substantiated by standard Korean sources, probably presents a generally accurate impression of the tactics used by some of the Tonghak rebel administrators:

> ... Governors, magistrates and other officers were deposed in summary order, many meeting swift justice for past misdeeds. The Tong Hak gained over the people in the following manner. A man clothed as a high official was sent to a village. He carried the royal seal of authority, *pyeng pou* [*pyŏngbu*], a reed given by the King to his messengers. This reed is broken, one half remaining in the Palace and the other being carried by the official. This intimated that there was royalty among the Tong Haks. This officer summoned the villagers before him and asked who were Tong Haks. The unwilling were then politely urged to join until the majority came over. These then were sent against the halting minority. If they failed, the officer summoned the stubborn one before him. He would not so much as see his face but the victim was made to kneel on the ground outside the officer's door and was told to join at once or take the consequence – death.[10]

Second Stage: Advance and Withdrawal

The northward movement of the rebellion was resumed in May, 1894, and by the first of June, Chŏn's consistently victorious forces had captured Chŏnju, the capital of Chŏlla Province and located in the northern part of the province, about 150 miles south of Seoul. General Hong Kye-hun, the Government Commander in the area, immediately moved his forces to Chŏnju and fought Chŏn's rebel army for seven days in an unsuccessful effort to recapture the city. Then Hong, realizing his inability to defeat the rebels and apparently seeking to gain time for planning new strategy, obtained an armistice agree-

---

[9]O Chi-yŏng, *Tonghak Sa* [History of Tonghak] (Seoul: Yŏngch'ang Sŏgwan, 1940) pp. 126-127.

[10]Junkin, *op. cit.*, p. 60.

ment from Chŏn, subject to the King's approval.[11] On June 11, General Hong asked the King for reinforcements and for the assistance of military forces from China. On June 14, General Hong, presumably on orders from the King, made the following three-point offer to Chŏn, on the condition that the latter evacuate Chŏnju and disband his forces:

(1) There will be no popular discrimination against Tonghak members. Anyone found guilty of such discrimination will be punished.
(2) All debts and mortgages of Tonghak members will be canceled.
(3) Tonghak members will be permitted unrestricted travel and protection from violence.[12]

Despite the obviously unrealistic nature of the second promise, in particular, Chŏn Pong-jun accepted the promises given him by General Hong in the name of the King. Although Chŏn did not disband his forces, he withdrew them from Chŏnju on June 14, 1894.

Chŏn's agreement to withdraw from a strong position without achieving his major objectives probably was motivated at least in part by a genuine spirit of patriotism. Chŏn apparently was disturbed over the fact that the Tonghak action had resulted in the entrance of foreign troops into Korea—a result inconsistent with Chŏn's objective of ridding the government of corrupting influences, foreign as well as domestic.[13] Other possible motivations were: (1) a desire to avoid further suffering among the people; and (2) uneasy relations between Chŏn's jurisdiction (Namjŏp) and the orthodox Tonghak jurisdiction (Pukchŏp). The Pukchŏp area extended almost to Chŏnju and blocked Chŏn's route northward.[14]

Korea Becomes an International Battleground

The first elements of Chinese forces, dispatched to Korea at the request of the Korean King, had arrived at Inch'ŏn on June 5. The Chinese Government notified the Japanese Government of this action *after* the troops had disembarked, rather than *prior to* their dispatch as stipulated in the Tientsin Convention of 1885. Japan then notified China on the 7th that Japanese troops were being sent to Korea, and these began to disembark on June 10.[15]

On June 24, the Korean Minister of Foreign Affairs officially requested the American Minister to make efforts to effect the withdrawal of Chinese and Japanese troops, on the ground that the Tonghak Rebellion, the ostensible

[11]*Ch'ŏndogyo Ch'ang Kŏn Sa*, Pt. II, p. 60.

[12]Kim Sang-gi, *op. cit.*, pp. 95-96.

[13]Yi Sŏn-gŭn, *op. cit.*, p. 178; *Tonghak Nan Kirok* [Records of the Tonghak Rebellion] (Seoul: Kuksa P'yŏnch'an Wiwŏnhoe, 1960), Vol. I, pp. 109-113; Vol. II, p. 538. In the latter source, Tonghak leaders are repeatedly quoted to the effect that ridding Korea of Japanese influence was the major objective of the Tonghak Rebellion.

[14]Kim Sang-gi, *op. cit.*, p. 96.

[15]Mr. Denby to Mr. Gresham, *Foreign Relations*, 1894, App. I, No. 17, pp. 24-25.

cause of the introduction of troops, had been ended.[16] The American Minister, in accordance with instructions from Washington, did institute multilateral conversations with the representatives of Great Britain, Russia, and France in Seoul, designed to bring about simultaneous withdrawal of Chinese and Japanese forces. A joint note urging such action was sent to the Chinese and Japanese representatives, but to no avail. China was willing to withdraw simultaneously, but Japan insisted upon prior institution of reforms by the Korean government and prior withdrawal of the Chinese forces.[17]

Great Britain's policy with respect to the Sino-Japanese difficulties was expressed as follows in the House of Commons by Sir Edward Grey, then Parliamentary Under Secretary of Foreign Office: "every effort which could properly be made by us will be used to bring about a friendly arrangement between them."[18] Britain sent notes to both China and Japan urging peace[19] and, through the British Minister in Peking, offered the good offices of Great Britain as a mediator.[20] This pacific, official British attitude continued despite the widespread popular indignation in England caused by the sinking by the Japanese, on July 25, of the British ship *Kowshing* transporting Chinese troops to Korea.[21] All efforts to maintain peace were unavailing, however, and on August 1, 1894, China and Japan declared war on each other.[22]

Prior to the outbreak of war, Japan had been exerting increasingly strong pressure on the Korean government, and on July 23 Japanese forces had seized the King's palace and made the King a virtual prisoner. After the declaration of war, Japan, on August 26, forced upon the Korean government a treaty of alliance against China, and thus replaced China as the controlling power in the country.[23]

In Japan, meanwhile, there were ultranationalist elements which felt that the Japanese government was moving too slowly against China and against the Chinese-supported Korean government. Earlier in 1894, Kim Ok-kyun, the prominent Korean reformer who had led the abortive revolt of 1884 and

---

[16]Korean Minister of Foreign Affairs to Mr. Sill, *Foreign Relations*, 1894, App. 1, Incl. 1 in No. 16, p. 23.

[17]Joint Note from the Foreign Representatives at Seoul to the Imperial Chinese and Japanese Representatives, *Ibid.*, Incl. 2 in No. 16, pp. 23-24; Mr. Denby to Mr. Gresham, *Ibid.*, No. 17, pp. 24-25; Mr. Sill to Mr. Gresham, *Ibid.*, No. 18, pp. 25-27 (with Incl. 1, Mr. Otori's reply to Joint Note and Incls. 2 and 3, Mr. Yüan's replies to Joint Note). See also English texts of notes exchanged between China and Japan prior to hostilities, in Vladimir (pseud.), *The China-Japan War* (London: Sampson Low, Marston, 1896), App. B, pp. 338-348.

[18]Hansard, *Parliamentary Debates* (Fourth Series), Vol. XXVI, July 5, 1894, p. 950.

[19]*Ibid.*, Vol. XXVII, July 30, 1894, p. 1263.

[20]Vladimir, *op. cit.*, p. 347, Komura to Chinese Foreign Office, July 4, 1894.

[21]Hansard (Fourth Series), Vol. XXVII, Aug. 2, 1894, p. 1573; *Ibid.*, Vol. XXVIII, Aug. 10, 1894, p. 569.

[22]Vladimir, *op. cit.*, App. D, pp. 370-374.

[23]For treaty text, see W. W. Rockhill (Ed.), *Treaties and Conventions With or Concerning China and Korea, 1894-1904* (Washington: Govt. Printing Office, 1904), p. 429.

had subsequently resided in Japan, was lured to Shanghai and murdered by an agent of his uncompromising political enemies, the ruling pro-Chinese Korean conservatives. When Kim's body was sent back to Korea, it was dismembered and displayed throughout the country as a gory warning to Korean "traitors" whose Japanese-supported reform efforts threatened the foundations of the conservatives' power position.[24] The Kim Ok-kyun incident aroused intense anti-Chinese feeling in Japan, particularly in the important ultra-nationalist group known as *Genyōsha* ("Dark Ocean Society"). Elements of this society unsuccessfully urged the Japanese government to use the incident as a pretext for launching an immediate attack on China.[25]

With the failure of this attempt to stir up Sino-Japanese hostilities and establish Japanese control in Korea, certain *Genyōsha* elements contacted Chŏn Pong-jun with a view to exploiting his Tonghak rebel movement for the same purposes. According to the best available evidence, however, the Japanese, after a careful evaluation of the rebel organization, determined that it would be of no value in the achievement of Japanese objectives, and abandoned the idea of collaborating with Chŏn Pong-jun. Moreover, acceptance of Japanese support by Chŏn — particularly after the landing of foreign troops and after his withdrawal from Chŏnju — would have been in direct conflict with his apparent objectives. In any event, there is no reliable evidence that the *Genyōsha* or any other Japanese group provided assistance to the Tonghak rebel forces.[26]

Third Stage: Reunification and Defeat

Until the fall of 1894, the Tonghak movement was clearly split between

---

[24] *Chosŏn Chi Wiin* [Eminent Koreans] (Seoul: Kaebyŏksa, 1926), p. 237.

[25] Min T'ae-wan, *Kapsin Chŏngbyŏn Kwa Kim Ok-kyun* [The 1884 Incident and Kim Ok-kyun] (Seoul: Kukche Munhwa Hyŏphoe, p. 57. Also, Kim Sang-gi, *op. cit.*, p. 103.

[26] Dean Yi Pyŏng-do of the Graduate School of Seoul National University, has reached this conclusion after extended research on the Tonghak movement.

There have been, however, noteworthy allegations of active Japanese involvement in the Tonghak Rebellion. Among Westerners in Seoul at the time of the Rebellion, it was a common belief that it had been fostered by the Japanese; one Western observer later declared without qualification that the rebels had been organized, equipped and trained by Japan as her "puppets," to give Japan an excuse for war against China. See F. A. McKenzie, *Korea's Fight For Freedom* (New York: Revell, 1920), pp. 44-45.

Numerous Korean and Japanese writers believe that the Japanese gave some sort of aid to Chŏn Pong-jun's rebels, although they have not been able to prove it. One Japanese writer presents an interesting and detailed, but unsubstantiated, account of active military assistance to Chŏn's forces on the part of a *Genyōsha*-affiliated group called *Tenyūkyō* ("Heaven-guided Group"). According to this account, the *Tenyūkyō* (*Ch'ŏnuhyŏp* in Korean), after earlier contacts with Chŏn, began its active assistance program shortly after Chŏn's withdrawal from Chonju. At this time, *Tenyūkyō* members allegedly revealed to Chŏn the falsity of a message, sent to him by the Chŏlla Provincial Governor and appealing to him, ostensibly in the name of the King, to disband his forces, which had resumed local operations in Chŏlla Province. The *Tenyūkyō* assistance allegedly consisted of the provision of some weapons (type and quantity unspecified) and a full staff of military advisors. The military organization reportedly was headed by Chŏn Pong-jun, who had the title of *Ch'ongdok* (Governor General) and who had three Japanese advisors. Under the top level, there were said to be the following commands, each with one or two Japanese advisors: (1) Guerrilla Forces: (2) East Front Forces; (3) West Front Forces; (4) South Front Forces; (5) North Front Forces; (6) Supply Forces; and (7) Red Cross. One of the principal figures among the *Tenyūkyō* members was said to be Uchida Ryōhei, the nationalist firebrand who, seven years later at the age of 27, established the notorious Black Dragon Society. Aoyagi Nammei, *Chōsen Shiwa to Shiseki* [Korean Historical Tales and Places] (5th ed.; Seoul: Korean Research Society, 1928), p. 743. See also *Dai Jimmei Jiten* [The Great Dictionary of Personal Names] Tokyo: Heibonsha, 1953), p. 872.

the orthodox and rebel organizations. This situation created serious handicaps for both groups. The efforts of Ch'oe Si-hyŏng, the *Sinsa*, to keep his orthodox elements aloof from the rebellion were largely unsuccessful since the Korean government, failing to grasp its opportunity to gain orthodox Tonghak support against the rebels, tended to hunt down Tonghak members without discrimination.[27] Moreover, the maintenance of *esprit de corps* and discipline within the *Sinsa's* organization became increasingly difficult, as indicated by the fact that the *Sinsa* considered it necessary to issue the following stern, eight-point directive in September, 1894:

1. The business of each *p'o* shall be done under orders from the officer in charge.

2. People who open up tombs and seize other people's property should be punished in accordance with Tonghak law.

3. Members of each *p'o* who take advantage of Tonghak influence to confiscate property should be severely punished.

4. Any interference by one *p'o* in the business of another *p'o* should be reported to the Legal Office.

5. A member of any *p'o* who convenes a meeting without written permission from the proper Tonghak officials will be expelled from the organization.

6. Any people who fight each other without reason will have their names publicly displayed and transmitted to every *p'o*.

7. Drunkenness and gambling are not proper conduct for followers of the Way. Anyone found guilty of these things will therefore be expelled.

8. The affairs of each *p'o*, whether of greater or lesser consequence, will be conducted in accordance with the instructions of the Tonghak sect.[28]

Chŏn Pong-jun's rebel forces were not only deprived of the added strength which the cooperation of the Pukchŏp forces would have given them, but were further weakened by the activities of opportunistic individuals within the local Pukchŏp leadership, particularly in Ch'ungch'ŏng Province, where advance elements of Chŏn's rebel forces were located. These Pukchŏp people, and even certain members of Chŏn's own forces, stole arms and enticed soldiers to move from one group to another in order to strengthen certain units and weaken others. Many new people (including the unemployed, local gentry, and even *yangban*), who had joined Chŏn's forces after the withdrawal from Chŏnju, were among those principally responsible for weakening Chon's rebel army; some of them betrayed the Tonghak movement by spying for the government forces.[29]

The truce between the government command and Chŏn Pong-jun's Tonghak rebels after the withdrawal from Chŏnju was an uneasy one from the start. The government did not honor its agreement to cease its suppressive policies against Tonghak, and Chŏn's forces, rather than disbanding as the agreement stipulated, resumed local military operations in Chŏlla Province almost im-

[27]Homer B. Hulbert, "The Religion of the Heavenly Way," *Korea Review*, Nov., 1906, pp. 418-424.

[28]*Ch'ŏndogyo Ch'ang Kŏn Sa*, Pt. II, pp. 63-65.

[29]Kang Chae-ŏn, *op. cit.*, No. 11, Nov. 1954, p. 24.

mediately after the withdrawal. During the autumn of 1894, the Korean government, with the support of Japanese troops, prepared to put down the Tonghak Rebellion by force. Chŏn Pong-jun, learning of these plans, prepared his forces for a new northward march.

Ch'oe Si-hyŏng, the *Sinsa,* looked upon Chŏn's battle preparations as a threat to the orthodox Tonghak organization (Pukchŏp), particularly in Ch'ungch'ŏng Province through which Chŏn's rebel forces would have to pass. The *Sinsa* therefore issued an official statement in which he said that the Namjŏp rebels, in violation of the Tonghak doctrine, were preparing to fight the orthodox Tonghaks of Pukchŏp. The statement further declared that Chŏn Pong-jun in Chŏlla Province and his associate Sŏ Chang-ok in Ch'ungch'ŏng Province were traitors to the state and heretics of the Tonghak faith. The *Sinsa* called upon all true Tonghaks to prepare to fight the Namjŏp rebels.

O Chi-yŏng, a Tonghak leader who was associated with Chŏn Pong-jun in the rebellion but who retained the respect of the orthodox leaders, quickly began to mediate the factional dispute. He visited three of the *Sinsa's* principal subordinates—Kim Yŏn-guk, Son Pyŏng-hi, and Son Ch'ŏn-min—and appealed to them, saying:

> According to our doctrine, it is not right to have a rebellion. Under present circumstances, however, it is not right to attack Chŏn, although he was wrong. Now, before Pukchŏp has begun to fight, the government, the Japanese, and even the Chinese have already opened their attack on the Namjŏp. It is clear that these forces will be able to defeat Namjŏp, so that the defeat would only be hastened if Pukchŏp forces were to fight with these others. But in this event, the Namjŏp forces, without thinking of their impotence against the enemy, would blame Pukchŏp for their defeat. Also, how could we Pukchŏp people face the world if we had allied ourselves with the strong side against the weaker? Let us not talk about who is right or wrong. Followers of the Way should cooperate with each other in life or death.[31]

O Chi-yŏng's arguments convinced Son Pŏng-hi and Son Ch'ŏn-min that the two factions should join forces. At a mass meeting of Tonghak members called by the *Sinsa* on October 16, 1894 at Ch'ŏngsan in Ch'ungch'ŏng Province, the *Sinsa's* two trusted advisors persuaded him to accept O Chi-yŏng's reasoning and join forces with Chŏn Pong-jun. Son Pyŏng-hi and Son Ch'ŏn-min further informed the *Sinsa* that the Tonghak people in Ch'ungch'ŏng Province and northward were only awaiting his orders to mobilize. The *Sinsa* thereupon issued his orders, declaring to all his followers that this was the proper time to mobilize and support Chŏn Pong-jun in redressing the wrong done to their former teacher, and instructing them to cooperate with Chŏn's rebel movement.[32]

Ch'oe Si-hyŏng, the *Sinsa,* now came to an agreement with Chŏn Pong-jun, and Chŏn made final plans for marching on Seoul in command of an official

---

[30]O Chi-yŏng, *op. cit.,* pp. 138-139.   [31]*Ibid.*
[32]*Ch'ŏndogyo Ch'ang Kŏn Sa,* Pt. II, pp. 63-65; O Chi-yŏng, *op. cit.,* p. 139.

Tonghak force, supported by Ch'oe and the Tonghak organization as a whole. In the latter part of October, this new Tonghak army marched northward into Ch'ungch'ŏng Province and captured Kongju, the provincial capital, about 100 miles south of Seoul. This advance, however, was the beginning of the end. The Tonghak forces were decisively defeated on November 29, 1894 by a composite force of Korean Government soldiers and highly trained and equipped Japanese troops. The rebellion was then quickly put down. Chŏn Pong-jun and his subordinate rebel leaders, and also many of the orthodox Tonghak leaders, were captured and, after peremptory trials, executed.[33]

Appraisal of Chŏn Pong-jun and the Tonghak Rebellion

Chŏn Pong-jun's character and his motivations in leading the Tonghak Rebellion are the subjects of controversy among Korean historians. One group regards Chŏn as a politically ambitious opportunist who felt that the weakening effects upon the government of domestic factionalism and foreign pressures had created a favorable opportunity for seizing power. This school holds that Chŏn was not a genuine Tonghak adherent but joined the movement in order to exploit its grass roots organization and its emotional fervor in the achievement of his political ambition. One fact cited in support of this contention is that Chŏn, in his pronouncements concerning the causes and objectives of the Tonghak Rebellion, did not mention the fundamental Tonghak aim of clearing the founder's name. It is further suggested by these writers that Chŏn had an agreement with the ruthless, power-hungry *Taewŏngun*, the former Regent, to use the rebellion as a screen for the latter's return to political control.[34]

Other recognized Korean historians consider Chŏn an outstanding patriot and a sincere Tonghak member, interested in establishing a utopia in accordance with Tonghak principles. These writers, though recognizing that engaging in rebellion was contrary to Tonghak doctrine, tend to justify Chŏn's action on the ground that unremitting government persecution had left the Tonghaks with no practical alternative to rebellion. This school also reasons that, though Chŏn and the *Taewŏngun* had many interests in common, their ultimate objectives were different, and that Chŏn, not being the type of person to permit himself to be used as the *Taewŏngun's* pawn, made no agreement with him.[35]

---

[33]Kim Sang-gi, *op. cit.*, pp. 108 ff.

[34]*Ibid.*, pp. 77-80. Professor Kim Sang-gi is one of the recognized Korean historians who hold these views about Chŏn Pong-jun. With respect to a possible understanding between Chŏn and the *Taewŏngun*, Professor Kim, though acknowledging the absence of complete proof, believes, on the basis of extensive questioning of Ch'ŏndogyo members and other informed persons, that there was such an agreement. In this connection, Mr. Heard, the American Minister, reported from Seoul on April 20, 1893 that "a few persons" considered it possible that the Tonghak movement was being used by the *Taewŏngun*. Mr. Heard to Mr. Gresham, *Foreign Relations*, 1894, App. I, No. 4, p. 11.

[35]O Chi-yŏng, *op. cit.*, pp. 138-139, 158; Kang Chae-ŏn, *op. cit.*, No. 11, Nov. 1954, pp. 14-15.

This position is supported by Chŏn's testimony at his trial following the Tonghak Rebellion.[36]

As has already been indicated, the use of armed force as an instrument for the achievement of Tonghak objectives was inconsistent with Tonghak doctrine. It was also politically inexpedient to adopt forceful methods as long as passive measures were achieving any degree of success in the face of continuing and increasing government persecution. For twenty-nine years (1863-1892), Ch'oe Si-Hyŏng, the *Sinsa,* persistently drove home to his followers these two basic reasons for employing only passive techniques. It was only after the ultracautious Ch'oe became convinced of the necessity of some direct action to save the movement that he permitted the use of even the intermediate device of formal petitioning of the government. From the standpoint of Ch'oe and his orthodox subordinates, therefore, the resort to armed force was an admission of at least temporary failure of the positive Tonghak program and was acceptable only as a negative step absolutely essential to the preservation of the Tonghak movement.

Chŏn Pong-jun had some grounds for feeling that Ch'oe and his orthodox associates were unduly cautious about taking countermeasures against the government. But in launching the rebellion in defiance of the principal Tonghak leadership, he not only acted counter to Tonghak principles but also precipitated the division of the formerly unified, effectively organized movement into two hostile camps at the very time when unity was most needed. His action, therefore, could hardly have been calculated to advance the Tonghak movement.

Chŏn's resort to armed force against the government could be more easily explained on the basis of the Sino-Korean tradition which recognized the right of revolution in the face of official oppression.[37] On the basis of this tradition, the extreme inequities of the government administration in the late 1800's toward the lower classes, and particularly toward the Tonghak movement, furnished reasonable justification for a rebellion.

Irrespective of motivation or justification, Chŏn Pong-jun and his forces achieved considerable success in employing the technique of armed rebellion. This success can be attributed principally to: (1) Chŏn's ability to capitalize

[36]Professor Yi Pyŏng-do has given the writer the following carefully considered statement on the relationship of Chŏn Pong-jun and the *Taewŏngun:* "Chŏn, in his trial, flatly denied any association with the *Taewŏngun.* However, in the trial of the *Taewŏngun*'s grandson, Yi Chun-yong, it was testified that some of Yi's followers had contacted the Tonghak forces (not necessarily Chŏn himself) by letter, proposing coordination of the Tonghaks' entry into Seoul with an uprising within Seoul, in order to stage a *coup d'état* and put Yi Chun-yong in power. Although there is no positive evidence that the *Taewŏngun* was directly involved, it appears almost certain that his power was behind his grandson."

The plot of the *Taewŏngun*'s grandson to utilize the Tonghak forces in effecting a *coup d'état* also appears in a "secret Japanese report" referred to by Prince Itō in his memoirs. Itō Hirobumi (Prince), *Chōsen Kōshō Shiryō* [Source Materials on Relations With Korea] (2 vols.; Tokyo: Hishō Ruisan Kankokai, 1936), Vol. I, p. 638.

[37]Homer B. Hulbert, "The Religion of the Heavenly Way," *Korea Review,* Dec. 1906, p. 460; Herrlee G. Creel, *Confucius, the Man and the Myth* (New York: John Day, 1949), pp. 268-269.

upon the deep-seated grievances of the Tonghak people against official corruption and oppression; and (2) the military skill of Chŏn and his associates in building an effective rebel fighting force from an impoverished, embittered, untrained peasantry.

There were a number of significant factors contributing to the failure of the rebellion. The adverse effects of the split in the Tonghak organization have already been discussed. The principal direct cause of the failure was the intervention of foreign forces. Chŏn had apparently had some opportunity to acquaint himself with the political and military situation in Seoul.[38] He was insufficiently informed on contemporary international politics relating to Korea, however, to realize that Japan would use an internal disturbance in Korea as a basis for intervening and eliminating Chinese influence in the country. A third factor was the primitive nature of Chŏn's weapons as compared with those of the opposing Japanese forces. Fourth, the opposition of the middle class (merchants, holders of small property, and people of moderate education) contributed significantly to Chŏn's failure. These people, unlike the socially and politically oppressed classes, accepted the government position that Tonghak thoughts were dangerous and that the Tonghak doctrine was a false religion. This attitude increased as the rebellion progressed and as predominantly unprincipled people joined the movement.[39]

Despite the failure of the Tonghak Rebellion militarily, it had the effect of demonstrating that the Korean rank and file were a force to be reckoned with by any rulers who persistently oppressed them. The principal significance of the Tonghak movement as a whole is that, as the first Korean reform movement with significant mass support and grass roots organization, it planted the seeds of popular reform among the Korean people.[40]

---

[38]Kim Sang-gi, *op. cit.*, p. 79; Kang Chae-ŏn, *op. cit.*, pp. 14-15; *Ch'ŏndogyo Ch'ang Kŏn Sa*, Pt. II, pp. 57-58.

[39]These factors are all discussed in Kim Sang-gi, *op. cit.*, p. 119. See also *Ch'ŏndogyo Ch'ang Kŏn Sa*, Pt. II, p. 70.

[40]Kim Sang-gi, *op. cit.*, p. 125.

CHAPTER V
EASTERN LEARNING AND THE RISING SUN

Conflicting Japanese and Russian Interests in Korea

In the Treaty of Shimonoseki of April, 1895 ending the Sino-Japanese War, China formally renounced its former special position in Korea and recognized the "full and complete independence and autonomy" of Korea. China also ceded to Japan the southern tip of the Liaotung Peninsula, including Port Arthur.[1] The Russian government, however, with the cooperation of France and Germany in the "Triple Intervention," was able to force Japan to return the Liaotung territory to China. This humiliating experience added new bitterness to Russo-Japanese relations, and caused Japan to exert strenuous efforts to build up its military strength to such a point that it would be able to block any similar future effort to intervene in its affairs.[2]

Japan, for a time, lost even its newly gained ascendency in Korea to Russia, as a result of the excesses of the Japanese "reformers" who went so far as to instigate the murder of the anti-Japanese Queen of Korea in October, 1895.[3] The Korean King then turned to Russia for support, and ruled the country from the Russian legation from February, 1896 to February, 1897. Meanwhile, Russia's reckless expansionism in Manchuria and North China led, in March, 1898, to the conclusion of a treaty between Russia and China in which the latter was obliged to cede to Russia for 25 years the ports of Talienwan and Port Arthur, the very area which Russia had forced Japan to return to China in 1895.[4] In view of the strong resentment aroused in Japan and also Britain by this audacious seizure, Russia apparently considered it politically necessary to assume a more conciliatory position in Korea. The result was the Nishi-Rosen Protocol of April, 1898, in which both Russia

---

[1] Rockhill, *op. cit.*, pp. 14-20.

[2] *Ibid.*, for text of Japan's formal recession of the territory. See also *Chōsen Shi Taikei* [Outline of Korean History] (Seoul: Chōsen Shi Gakkai. 1927), Vol. IV, p. 128; also Langer, *op. cit.*, p. 897.

[3] E. Satow to Marquess of Salisbury, March 26, 1898, in Gooch and Temperley (Eds.), *British Documents on the Origins of the War*, Vol. I, pp. 25-27. Also see Clarence N. Weems, Jr., *op. cit.*, pp. 138-147.

[4] Rockhill, *op. cit.*, pp. 50-52.

and Japan reaffirmed their respect for Korean independence and agreed not to interfere in Korean internal affairs.[5]

The interests of Russia and Japan in Korea, however, were in basic conflict, and neither government showed an inclination to make the concessions prerequisite to a permanent settlement. Japan, moving to strengthen its position against Russia, received assurances of benevolent neutrality from the United States and Britain. In addition, the Anglo-Japanese Alliance of January, 1902, committed Britain to render active assistance to Japan, should another power join Russia in war against Japan. France, Russia's European ally, assumed a position of neutrality relative to any Russo-Japanese hostilities. Germany, the other major European power which might then have sided with Russia, also maintained a neutral position.[6]

By 1902, Russia, having become convinced that control of the Korean (Tsushima) Straits was needed to provide free passage between the Russian-held ports of Port Arthur and Vladivostok, exerted new pressure on the Korean Government, at the expense of the Japanese position in Korea. Russo-Japanese negotiations, which were resumed in August, 1903, were fruitless, and war broke out on February 8, 1904.[7]

Son Pyŏng-hi Assumes Tonghak Leadership

With the crushing of the Tonghak Rebellion in 1894, the leadership and organization of the Tonghak movement had been virtually destroyed. However, Son Pyŏng-hi, who had been the principal protegé of Ch'oe Si-hyŏng, the *Sinsa,* managed to escape arrest and execution. Ch'oe himself evaded arrest for almost four years, and personally turned over the position of top leader of Tonghak to Son Pyŏng-hi. According to the official record in the Tonghak history, Son, in the summer of 1898 — shortly after the signature of the Nishi-Rosen Protocol between Japan and Russia — was led by a dream to the hiding place of Ch'oe. The *Sinsa,* who was anticipating arrest by the Korean government authorities, asked Son to succeed him, and breathed into his successor's mouth as a symbol of the transfer of leadership. A few days later, Ch'oe was convicted and executed in Seoul. When Son Pyŏng-hi assumed the leadership, he was known by the honorific name, Uiam, and bore the ecclesiastic title of *Sŏngsa,* or Holy Teacher.[8]

[5]C. N. Weems, *op. cit.,* pp. 452 ff.; Satow to Marquess of Salisbury, *op. cit.,* pp. 25-27; Dallin, *op. cit.,* pp. 49-50; Baron Rosen, *Forty Years of Diplomacy* (London: George Allen and Unwin, 1922), pp. 159-161. For text, see Rockhill, *op. cit.,* p. 433.

[6]For text of Anglo-Japanese Treaty, see Rockhill, *op. cit.,* pp. 97-98; for President Roosevelt's policy of benevolent neutrality, see Roosevelt to Sternburg, *Die Grosse Politik,* Vol. XIX, Pt. I, No. 5992, quoted in A.L.P. Dennis, *Adventures in American Diplomacy, 1896-1906* (New York: Dutton, 1928), p. 364; Roosevelt to Kennan, quoted in Tyler Dennett, *Roosevelt and the Russo-Japanese War* (New York: Doubleday, Page, 1925), pp. 160-161; Baron Eckardstein to Baron Rothschild, Jan. 12, 1904, cited in Edward H. Zabriskie, *American-Russian Rivalry in the Far East* (Philadelphia: Univ. of Penna. Press, 1946), pp. 101-102.

[7]For text of Japanese declaration of war against Russia, see Carnegie Endowment for International Peace, Pamphlet No. 43, *Korea: Treaties and Agreements* (Washington, 1921), pp. 52-53.

[8]*Ch'ŏndogyo Ch'ang Kŏn Sa,* Pt. III, p. 14.

The Third Great Leader of Ch'ŏndogyo,
Son Pyŏng-hi
(Official Ch'ŏndogyo Portrait)

Son Pyŏng-hi, like the Tonghak founder Ch'oe Che-u and many other Tonghak members, was in the socially inferior class of sons of concubines. He accordingly shared the traditional Tonghak interest in eliminating discriminatory practices in Korean society and government. As has been seen, Son had long been a devout believer in the Tonghak doctrine and had remained firmly loyal to Ch'oe Si-hyŏng throughout the period when Chŏn Pong-jun and other advocates of revolutionary tactics had split the movement by launching the Tonghak Rebellion. When Son Pyŏng-hi acquired the *Sinsa's* mantle of leadership, therefore, he insisted that the Tonghak movement devote itself to nonviolent activity, as before the rebellion.[9]

Son Pyŏng-hi, the *Sŏngsa*, spent most of his first three years in office rebuilding the shattered Tonghak organization, revitalizing the spiritual life of the movement, and consolidating his own position of control. In the spring of 1899, for example, he gave recognition to the leadership potential of Pak In-ho by formally ordaining him and giving him the honorific name, *Ch'unam*. In the summer of 1899, the *Sŏngsa* wrote a new doctrinal work entitled *Kakse Chin'gyŏng* (Code of Enlightenment), which applied the principle of *In nae ch'ŏn* (Man and God are one) to matter as well as to the human mind and spirit. He also taught Tonghak members about the providence of God, and emphasized the importance of giving thanks to God for life, food, and the other blessings of life. During the year 1899, he proclaimed a fast, proscribing the use of fish, meat, and tobacco. According to the official Tonghak record, when members of the *Sŏngsa's* own household disregarded his order and ate fish, they became seriously ill; by touching their hands, however, he cured them of their ailments and also of their tendency to disobey!

In the early summer of 1900, when most of the principal Tonghak leaders were gathered together for the reburial of the remains of Ch'oe Si-hyŏng, the *Sŏngsa* requested them to demonstrate their support for him by re-ordaining him. He had reason to feel that some of the leaders had not fully accepted him as their leader, despite his having received the leadership commission directly from the late *Sinsa*. Though he accepted the unanimous view of the leaders that a new ordination was unnecessary, he donned the robe of Tonghak leader in their presence, and thereupon assumed the special title of *Pŏp Taedoju* (Supreme Leader of the Way).[10]

By the spring of 1901, Son Pyŏng-hi apparently felt that the Tonghak movement, though still persecuted by the government, was firmly re-established, and that his position of control was secure. From that time until the early part of 1906, he resided almost continuously in Japan. Available evidence does not show that Son was either forced to leave Korea or enticed by the Japanese. The records clearly reveal, however, that he was not on good terms with the Korean authorities and that he considered it advantageous for Tonghak to

[9]*Ibid.*, pp. 1-14.   [10]*Ibid.*, pp. 17-25.

associate itself with Japan, a nation then widely identified with reform and progress. While in Japan, Son devoted major attention to a study of contemporary international affairs, with a view to determining the most effective role for the Tonghak organization to play in terms of Korean national interests. He also instituted a program of training in Japan for Tonghak youth.

The *Sŏngsa*'s first trip to Japan, in 1901, was a brief one, spent in Osaka. He took with him his brother, Son Pyŏng-hŭm, and his principal lieutenant, Yi Yong-gu. In 1902, Son returned to Japan, leaving Yi Yong-gu in active charge of the movement in Korea. During this stay, Son resided at the restful cultural center of Nara, and it was apparently here that he received most of the Tonghak leaders who came from Korea to confer with him in Japan.[11]

Son Pyŏng-hi as a Strategist

In 1903, while in Japan, Son became aware of the possibility of war between Japan and Russia. He considered that the time was ripe for a change in Korea, where the government was under predominantly Russian influence but where the Japanese bid for dominance remained strong. Son discussed the prospects for Korea with some of his leading followers, who were then with him in Japan. He reasoned as follows:

A war between Russia and Japan will be a war involving Manchuria and Korea. If Japan wins, Korea will be under Japanese domination; if Russia wins, Korea will be dominated by Russia. This point is as clear as light. So, if the Korean government stands idly by, it is plain enough that Korea will be ruined. If I were an official in the Korean government, I would have the following plan. First of all, if Russia and Japan opened hostilities, we must know who would win. After reaching that decision, we must commit troops in alliance with the country destined to win, in order to obtain the position of a victorious country. After obtaining that status, we must exploit it at the peace conference in order to secure a treaty which will protect the security of our country. This is our only chance of all time.

In my opinion, a Japanese victory can be definitely predicted for the following reasons:

(1) Russia is obviously at a disadvantage from the point of view of geographical position.

(2) There is very little enthusiasm for war in Russia, since Russia's only objective in fighting a war is to obtain an unfrozen port thousands of miles from home. With respect to the Japanese, however, this is a war at the risk of their lives, and the spiritual motivation is stronger. This point will make the difference between victory and defeat.

(3) There is also the problem of military strategy and weapons. In this regard, present-day Japan is different from the Japan of the Sino-Japanese War, because she has adopted German military tactics and weapons. This point cannot be ignored.

Therefore, the Korean position is to declare war against Russia and to obtain the position of a victorious nation. This is the most desirable course.[12]

As a first step toward implementing this policy, the *Sŏngsa* and the followers with him in Japan devised a scheme for driving the pro-Russian Korean faction from power in Seoul. The Tonghak organization would give support to Japan-

[11]*Ibid.*, pp. 27-43; also, Watanabe, *op. cit.*, pp. 21-22.

[12]*Ch'ŏndogyo Ch'ang Kŏn Sa*, Pt. III, pp. 32-34.

ese soldiers who would land at Korean treaty ports in the disguise of merchants, and the Tonghak elements and the Japanese forces would then make a co-ordinated attack on Seoul. The *Sŏngsa*'s brother, Son Pyŏng-hŭm, went to Korea to obtain reactions to the plan, and received support for it from all the principal Tonghak leaders there. Moreover, the proposed plan was given particularly enthusiastic endorsement by General Tamura, the commander of Japanese troops stationed in Korea. Both Son Pyŏng-hŭm and General Tamura died suddenly, however, before the plan could be carried out.[13]

The Sŏngsa thereupon abandoned this bold proposal and, late in 1903, submitted a petition to the President of the Cabinet (Premier) of the Korean Government, with a view to effecting governmental reforms consistent with Tonghak views concerning Korea's international position. In the petition, Son expressed concern about rumors which he had heard to the effect that the Korean Emperor might again take up residence in the Russian legation in Seoul, as he had done during the 1896-1897 period after the Japanese-instigated murder of the Queen. Son declared that if this should happen, the twenty million Koreans would be wandering aimlessly, "like sons without parents." On the other hand, he said, a united Korean nation, though small and without modern weapons, could rise up and drive out any foreign enemy. Secondly, the *Sŏngsa* cautioned that, in the event of war between Russia and Japan, Korea would be a battleground, and that the government should therefore exercise great care in choosing sides. The Tonghak leader stated, as a third point, that in the rise and fall of nations, the republic, the constitutional monarchy, and the absolute monarchy had all shown themselves to have both advantages and disadvantages. Irrespective of the form of government used, he said, the most important requirement was for an able executive with the judgment to make distinctions between important and less important matters. Son Pyŏng-hi concluded his petition by declaring that the Korean Government was faced with the three urgent problems of financial administration, administration of religion, and administration of diplomacy. If these three matters were taken care of, he said, all of Korea's important difficulties could be settled. Son implored the Premier to take timely action to save Korea from "disaster," but these views and recommendations of the *Sŏngsa* went unheeded.[14]

Ch'ŏndogyo and the Russo-Japanese War

When the Russo-Japanese War began on February 8, 1904, the Japanese immediately occupied Seoul and began the elimination of all Russian influence. On February 23, Japan forced on the Korean Government an agreement which legalized the new Japanese position. This protocol committed the Korean government to "adopt the advice" of Japan with respect to "improvements of administration," and bound Japan to "ensure the safety and repose of the Imperial House of Korea" and "definitively guarantee the independence and

---

[13]*Ibid.*   [14]*Ibid.*, pp. 34-42.

territorial integrity of the Korean Empire." Japan also acquired sweeping emergency powers which were to take effect whenever "the welfare of the Imperial House of Korea or the territorial integrity of Korea is endangered by aggression of a third power or internal disturbances." No direct reference was made to the Russo-Japanese hostilities then in progress.[15]

In the spring of 1904, shortly after the outbreak of the Russo-Japanese War, Son moved to Tokyo, presumably to have a better vantage point from which to follow and evaluate the war developments. At about this time, he made a donation of 10,000 yen (about $5,000) to the Japanese War Ministry.

During the opening month of the war, the *Sŏngsa* held a conference in Tokyo with forty of the top Tonghak leaders with a view to determining the course to be followed, under the circumstances, by the Tonghak organization. The *Sŏngsa* declared that there were three possible courses for them: (1) revolt: (2) instigation of drastic governmental and social reforms in Korea; and (3) active participation on the side of Japan in the war against Russia. The last, he said, was the only alternative promising any success. He specified, however, that Koreans (and Tonghak members in particular) should give assistance to Japan in such a way as to gain concessions which would insure Tonghak control of the Korean government after the war.

The principal result of this conference was that the Tonghak leaders, after their return to Korea, formed, in April, 1904, the *Taedong Hoe* (Great East Society). The *Sŏngsa* ordered members of the new society to cut off their hair (as a symbol of equality and progress). In July of the same year, the leaders met again and, for reasons which are obscure, changed the name of the society to *Chungnip Hoe* (Neutrality Society). A plan was also developed at this time to establish branches throughout the country. However, the Korean government retained its suspicions of the Tonghak movement. Despite the strong Japanese influence on the government, the Korean authorities arrested many members of the Tonghak-sponsored group, and eventually executed some of them.[16]

The *Sŏngsa*, still in Japan, heard of the suppressive action by the government, and discussed the situation with several principal Tonghak leaders. He ordered the name of the society changed to *Chinbo Hoe* (Progressive Society), and dispatched to it a statement of basic principles, a platform, and regulations. The basic principles were: (1) respect for the Throne and strengthening of national independence; (2) governmental reform; (3) reorganization of the military and financial systems; and (4) protection of life and property of the people.

The society then established local branches throughout the country and conducted an extensive membership campaign. Members were distinguished

---

[15]Rockhill, *op. cit.*, p. 441.

[16]*Ch'ŏndogyo Ch'ang Kŏn Sa*, Pt. III, pp. 43-44.

by their short haircuts and their black clothing. The *Chinbo Hoe* worked actively for government reform, and the Korean government, upon discovering that the new society was of Tonghak origin, took some initial steps to suppress it. Nevertheless, the government, desiring to profit by earlier mistakes, and perhaps responding to pressure from its Japanese "advisors," decided to initiate certain minor reforms itself, rather than waiting until forced to do so.[17]

During 1904, another reformist society known as the *Yusin Hoe* (Renewal Society) was established by the remaining members of the *Tongnip Hyŏphoe* (Independence Club) which had been organized in 1896 by Dr. Philip Jaisohn and other Japanese- and American-oriented Korean reformists. The *Yusin Hoe* later changed its name to *Ilchin Hoe* (Advancement Society) and operated by virtue of Japanese Army support.

The leaders of the *Ilchin Hoe*, expressing pleasure at the progress being made by the *Chinbo Hoe* and noting the apparent similarity of the objectives of the two societies, proposed a merger. The two groups were then united under the name *Ilchin Hoe*. Although Yun Si-pyŏng, the former leader of the *Ilchin Hoe*, remained as titular head, Yi Yong-gu, the *Sŏngsa's* chief lieutenant and former head of the *Chinbo Hoe*, became the actual leader of the new united society. Under Yi Yong-gu's leadership, the *Ilchin Hoe* established branch offices in thirteen principal centers in Korea, and used its influence in the investigation of official abuses and the correction of illegal tax practices. In addition, the society, under the direction of Yi Yong-gu, provided laborers to the Japanese armed forces during the Russo-Japanese War for the construction of the railroad in northwestern Korea and for the transportation of supplies in northeastern Korea. When Son Pyŏng-hi, the *Sŏngsa,* heard of this active assistance to the Japanese forces by the *Ilchin Hoe,* he was disturbed. It was too late, however, for him to take any corrective action.[18]

Aftermath of the War

Japan won the war against Russia, and in the Treaty of Portsmouth (September 5, 1905), gained Russia's recognition of Japan's "paramount political, military, and economical interests" in Korea.[19] On November 17, 1905, Japan forced upon the Korean government a treaty giving Japan control of Korean foreign relations and thereby creating a Japanese protectorate over Korea.[20]

Japan was able to conclude the protectorate treaty not only with the acquiescence of Russia, but with the full concurrence of the other interested powers. On August 12, 1905, a new Anglo-Japanese Agreement, superseding that of

[17]*Ibid.*, pp. 45-50.

[18]*Ibid.*, pp. 50-53. A closely parallel account is given by the Japanese historian Watanabe (Watanabe, *op. cit.*, pp. 26-33).

[19]W. W. Rockhill (Compiler), *Treaties, Conventions, Agreements, Ordinances, Etc. Relating to China and Korea, October, 1904-January, 1908* (Washington: Govt. Printing Office, 1908), pp. 150-155.

[20]*Ibid.*, pp. 276-277.

January 30, 1902, was concluded. In return for Japanese recognition of Great Britain's "special interest" in the area of India, Britain made the following commitment:

> Japan possessing paramount political, military, and economic interests in Corea, Great Britain recognizes the right of Japan to take such measures of guidance, control, and protection in Corea as she may deem proper and necessary to safeguard and advance those interests, provided always that such measures are not contrary to the principle of equal opportunities for the commerce and industry of all nations.[21]

On September 9, 1905, the French Foreign Minister, when shown a text of this new British acknowledgment of Japan's "paramount interests" in Korea, stated that he saw nothing in it to which France could take exception.[22] The United States also agreed to the protectorate, as indicated by the following statement of President Theodore Roosevelt to the American Ambassador to Russia during the Russo-Japanese War: "Japan ought to have a protectorate over Korea (which has shown its utter inability to stand by itself), and ought to succeed to Russia's right in and around Port Arthur . . ."[23]

Yi Yong-gu and other actively pro-Japanese Koreans immediately declared in favor of the Japanese protectorate. In response to questioning by Son Pyŏng-hi, Yi Yong-gu explained his action by stating that Korea, with the protection of Japan, would eventually gain complete independence. Son strongly renounced Yi's position, declaring:

> If we wish to have [Japanese] protection, we must abandon independence. If we wish to obtain independence, we must give up protection. Why, therefore, do you wish to obtain independence under the name of protection?[24]

Although Son Pyŏng-hi, the *Sŏngsa,* did not pursue this matter further at this time, the lines were clearly drawn for an early break between Son and the pro-Japanese Tonghak faction headed by Yi Yong-gu. The split did not actually occur until the following year, when Son returned from Japan to resume active leadership of his organization. The Tonghak period of the sect's history ended, however, on December 1, 1905, when the *Sŏngsa* ordered the name changed from Tonghak to Ch'ŏndogyo.[25]

---

[21]*Ibid.,* p. 113. For British diplomatic correspondence leading to the insertion of this article in the treaty, see Sir C. MacDonald to the Marquess of Lansdowne, July 8, 1905; Same to Same, July 15, 1905; Marquess of Lansdowne to Sir C. MacDonald, July 19, 1905; and Marquess of Lansdowne to Sir F. Bertie, Sept. 6, 1905 in *British Documents on the Origins of the War,* Vol. IV, pp. 145-151; 174.

[22]Sir F. Bertie to Marquess of Lansdowne, Sept. 9, 1905, *Ibid.,* p. 177.

[23]Dennett, *op. cit.,* pp. 161-162. See also Secretary Root to Min Yeung-Tchan, Special Envoy without Credentials, *Foreign Relations,* 1905, pp. 629-630 for the United States position that the Japanese protectorate over Korea had a legally recognized basis and that United States–Korean relations would accordingly be conducted through Japan.

[24]*Ch'ŏndogyo Ch'ang Kŏn Sa,* Pt. III, p. 53. The word translated "protection" is the general word *poho,* but, in the context, it might also be read as "protectorate."

[25]*Ibid.,* pp. 53 f.

Appraisal of Tonghak Collaboration with Japan

As has been seen, disagreement within the Tonghak leadership over the character and extent of cooperation with Japan led to a widening split in the organization after the establishment of the Japanese protectorate at the end of 1905. However, from the time that Son Pyŏng-hi first went to Japan in 1901 until about the end of the Russo-Japanese war (fall, 1905), there was essential agreement on the desirability of cooperation with Japan and on most of the particular methods to be employed.

The first of three tactics devised was that of active Tonghak support of Japanese clandestine operations against the antireformist, pro-Russian Korean Government. As has been stated above, this tactic was never put into practice, because of the sudden death of Son Pyŏng-hi's brother and the Japanese general, the two principals involved. However, the very fact that the *Sŏngsa* and the Tonghak leaders in Korea chose this tactic as a step toward achieving desired changes in the Korean government is worthy of note. The contemplated action, in which Tonghak elements would actively assist in a Japanese military coup, was inconsistent, in principle, with the *Sŏngsa*'s opposition to the technique of armed rebellion as employed by Chŏn Pong-jun in the Tonghak Rebellion. The new approach was based on Son Pyŏng-hi's conviction that Japan was destined to win the impending contest with Russia for control of Korea. For this reason, he felt that the best interests of Tonghak and of Korea itself lay in rendering Japan such military and other assistance as might be required to place Korea in the position of a victorious ally. It must, therefore, be concluded that the *Sŏngsa* was not actually opposed to the use of force on the basis of Tonghak principles, but rather on the basis of cold realism. He rejected the particular method in which Chŏn Pong-jun had employed armed force because Chŏn's rebellion had been unsuccessful. Son apparently reasoned that this lack of success had been due to Chŏn's ignorance of international politics and his resultant failure to effect a profitable alliance. Son advocated the use of armed force in alliance with Japan, because he felt that such action promised success for the Tonghak movement and for Korea.

One is justified in wondering why Son Pyŏng-hi permitted the projected Japanese-Tonghak joint operations plan to be abandoned simply because the original figures died unexpectedly. The nature of the plan and its timing (prior to the outbreak of war) were such as to justify a hope that the pro-Russian regime could have been driven from power under circumstances favorable to the acquisition of significant influence by the Tonghak movement. Only action of this type, on a large and dramatic scale, was likely to achieve the *Sŏngsa*'s aim of gaining objectives beneficial to Korea in alliance with Japan.

With respect to the tactic of petitioning the pro-Russian Korean Government, it seems certain that the *Sŏngsa* and his associates could not have entertained hope of achieving any positive result from this action. This Korean government was just as resistant to reform as had been the ruling group which, immediately prior to the Tonghak Rebellion, had given only empty promises in response to Tonghak petitions, or else had refused to receive the petitions altogether. The most logical explanation of this new petitioning action is that it was a psychological move, designed to establish a justification for the next tactical step.

The third tactic—formation of a Korean political action society—was initiated during the first month of the Russo-Japanese War, February, 1904. Under the first two designations *(Taesong Hoe* and *Chungnip Hoe)*, the Tonghak-sponsored society apparently made little headway. After it became known as the *Chinbo Hoe* (Progressive Society), this political action group adopted a simple, direct platform, established a nation-wide organization, and achieved some success in arousing public interest in its program and in goading the government into initiating at least superficial reform measures. The value of the society as an arm of Tonghak, however, was short-lived. Just as the *Chinbo Hoe* was showing promise of significant achievements, Son Pyŏng-hi's erstwhile protegé Yi Yong-gu led the group into a merger with the Japanese-supported *Ilchin Hoe* (Advancement Society), which was devoted to working for reforms in the interests of Japan rather than Korea.

CHAPTER VI
THE PURGE AND THE GREAT UPRISING

Japan Consolidates Its Control in Korea

Events proved the soundness of Son Pyŏng-hi's conviction that Japanese "protection" and Korean independence were incompatible. After forcing the protectorate treaty of November, 1905, on the Korean government, Japan steadily strengthened its control over the country. Early in 1906, Marquis (later Prince) Itō Hirobumi, one of the ablest and most enlightened leaders of Meiji Japan, was appointed the Japanese Resident-General in Korea with powers making him the virtual ruler of the country.[1] Although Itō's policies were generally moderate and were designed to effect a gradual reform and modernization of the Korean government and nation, they were clearly policies formulated and supported by an authoritarian Japanese government bent upon the achievement of Japanese, rather than Korean, objectives in Korea. There were continuous and widespread unrest and violence among the Koreans, aimed at the Korean government which had apparently sold out to the Japanese and also at Ch'ŏndogyo because of the close association of the sect with the now notoriously pro-Japanese *Ilchin Hoe.*

The transitional period of 1894-1905, much of which was characterized by Tonghak association with Japan, was clearly unsuccessful for the Tonghak (Ch'ŏndogyo) movement. Son Pyŏng-hi, the *Sŏngsa,* was a patriotic, but still politically immature, realist who was attempting to further the objectives of the Tonghak movement by emphasizing its nationalistic aspects. But although his analysis of existing domestic and international political conditions was sound in many respects, he was unable to capitalize on these conditions to achieve success for the movement. This failure must be attributed in large part to the great difficulties imposed on any such movement by the strong, conflicting influences of rival powers in Korea at that time. The *Sŏngsa* must be given the blame, however, for failing to develop a clear, effective position on collaboration with Japan and for losing control of his organization to unreliable, actively pro-Japanese elements. As will be seen in the following chapter, this

---

[1]Imperial Ordinance No. 267, Dec. 20, 1905, "Organization of the Residency-General and Residencies," (translation). Inclosure in unofficial note of Japanese Chargé in Washington to Secretary of State, Jan. 19, 1906, *Foreign Relations,* 1906, Pt. 2, pp. 1024-1026. See also Chargé Wilson to the Secretary of State, No. 389, Feb. 13, 1906, with Inclosures 1-4 (newspaper clippings reporting Marquis Itō's statement of his Korea policies prior to assuming the Residency-General), *Ibid.,* pp. 1027-1033.

latter error was particularly costly and led to a major reorientation of the Ch'ŏndogyo movement.

In 1907, the Korean Emperor (a title assumed, ironically, during the waning years of Korea's independence) made a final, unsuccessful attempt to gain international support for Korea's cause by dispatching a delegation secretly to the Second World Peace Congress at The Hague. In the same year, the Emperor abdicated under Japanese pressure and was succeeded by his young son who was powerless in Japanese hands. Japan, on the basis of a new agreement forced upon the Korean government on July 24, 1907, assumed almost complete control of Korea's domestic policies by placing Japanese officials in the administration.[2] In addition, the Japanese authorities ordered the disbanding of the Korean armed forces. This latter action resulted immediately in widespread insurrection, led by Korean Army remnants organized into a guerrilla force known as the *uibyŏngdae* (Righteous Army).[3] This anti-Japanese force continued its fight for several years and, in the course of its operations, killed many Ch'ŏndogyo members because, despite the fact that all connections between Ch'ŏndogyo and the pro-Japanese *Ilchin Hoe* had been severed by this time, the sect was still identified in the minds of many Korean nationalists with traitorous pro-Japanese activity.

In June, 1909, after more than three years as Resident-General, Prince Itō resigned, confessing failure to accomplish his Korean reform program;[4] in October of the same year, Itō was assassinated by a Korean nationalist. Formal annexation of Korea to Japan followed on August 22, 1910, with the acquiescence of the principal powers.[5] An extensive Japanese program of governmental reorientation, economic development, and attempted racial assimilation then began, under the stern direction of General Terauchi, the first Governor-General of Korea. As a part of the assimilation effort, all Korean social organizations, including the pro-Japanese *Ilchin Hoe,* were dissolved.

[2]The text of this agreement (translated) is Enclosure in note of Japanese Ambassador to Secretary of State, *Foreign Relations,* 1907, Pt. 2. pp. 773-774.

[3]Charge Dodge to Secretary of State, No. 417, Sept. 20, 1907, with Enclosure 1 (translated newspaper report of a speech by Marquis Itō referring to "riotous risings in the different parts of the country"), *Ibid.,* pp. 774-775.

[4]Sir C. MacDonald to Sir Edward Grey, No. 365, May 13, 1909, reporting conversation with Prince Itō in which he stated his intention to resign, *British Documents on the Origins of the War, 1898-1914,* Vol. VIII, p. 468. See also Roy H. Akagi, *Japan's Foreign Relations,* (Tokyo: Hokuseido, 1937), p. 279.

[5]For British Diplomatic papers on annexation, see Nos. 390-404, May 12-Oct. 10, 1910, *British Documents on the Origins of the War, 1898-1914,* Vol. VIII, pp. 487-502; text of treaty of annexation (translation) is given as Enclosure in No. 400, Baron Kato to Sir Edward Grey, Aug. 23, 1910.

For U.S. diplomatic sources, see documents headed "Administration of Affairs in Korea," *Foreign Relations,* 1910, pp. 677-685; the Declaration of the Japanese Government and the treaty are Enclosures 1 and 2, Japanese Ambassador to Acting Secretary of State, Aug. 24, 1910.

Russia's agreement to the annexation had been assured by the conclusion, on July 4, 1910, of a new Russo-Japanese treaty by which Russia recognized Japan's special interests in Korea, southern Manchuria, and eastern Inner Mongolia, and Japan acknowledged Russian dominance in northern Manchuria and Outer Mongolia. *Grosse Politik,* Vol. XXXII, p. 121.

Ch'ŏndogyo itself was permitted to continue, however, in the name of freedom of religion.[6]

The Sŏngsa's Purge of Pro-Japanese Elements

In the meantime, Son Pyŏng-hi, the *Sŏngsa*, had returned to Korea from Japan in February, 1906, and had immediately begun to reassert his direct leadership over the Ch'ŏndogyo organization. From the political point of view, the most urgent requirement for Son was the complete dissociation of the sect from the *Ilchin Hoe*, which, as has been seen, had become completely discredited in the eyes of patriotic Koreans.

Early in 1906, the *Sŏngsa* discussed the *Ilchin Hoe* with his subordinates Yi Yong-gu and Song Pyŏng-jun, stating that many Ch'ŏndogyo members had become so active in *Ilchin Hoe* affairs that they had neglected the basic principle of *sa in yŏ ch'ŏn* (treat people as though they were God) and had become general troublemakers. The *Sŏngsa* went on to say that the *Ilchin Hoe* organization had expanded so greatly in local areas that individuals who were members of both the *Ilchin Hoe* and Ch'ŏndogyo were interfering actively in local politics. Such Ch'ŏndogyo people, concluded the *Sŏngsa*, had abused their positions as members of the *Ilchin Hoe* and brought upon Ch'ŏndogyo the condemnation of the whole country. The *Sŏngsa* thereupon requested of Yi Yong-gu and Song Pyŏng-jun that they abolish all branch offices of the *Ilchin Hoe* and retain only the headquarters in Seoul. This request was ignored. On September 17, 1906, the *Sŏngsa* called Yi and Song again and impressed upon them the fact that the *Ilchin Hoe* had degenerated to such a point that anyone associated with the society was coming to be regarded as a traitor. Under existing circumstances, the *Sŏngsa* said, the Ch'ŏndogyo organization could no longer maintain any association with the *Ilchin Hoe* because: (1) the people had already come to regard the society as a traitorous organization; and (2) the nation was so unstable that the society could not achieve its avowed purpose of strengthening the nation. For these reasons, declared the *Sŏngsa*, all Ch'ŏndogyo members must divorce themselves from the *Ilchin Hoe* and devote themselves to orthodox Ch'ŏndogyo activities.

When Yi Yong-gu and Song Pyŏng-jun again ignored the *Sŏngsa*'s demands, these two rebellious leaders and some sixty other individuals who were prominent in both Ch'ŏndogyo and the *Ilchin Hoe* were expelled from Ch'ŏndogyo. The *Sŏngsa* thereby lost virtually all of his experienced leaders. Moreover, the expellees organized a rival cult called *Sich'ŏngyo* ("Serve Heaven Cult," a name derived from two key characters in Ch'oe Che-u's Sacred Formula) and utilized *Ilchin Hoe* groups to attack Ch'ŏndogyo and the *Sŏngsa*'s activities. *Sich'ŏngyo* also acquired title to all Ch'ŏndogyo property, since the former Ch'ŏndogyo treasurer, to whom permanent custody of the property had been

---

[6]For general coverage of developments reviewed in the foregoing section and for specific material on Ch'ŏndogyo implications, see *Ch'ŏndogyo Ch'ang Kŏn Sa*, Pt. II, p. 65; Henry Chung, *The Case of Korea* (New York: Revell, 1921), pp. 57-60; and McKenzie, *op. cit.*, pp. 104-170.

given by the *Sŏngsa,* was among those expellees who formed the rival cult. The *Sŏngsa* then dispatched messages to Ch'ŏndogyo groups throughout the country, urging members to beware of the blandishments of the new splinter group and to remain faithful to Ch'ŏndogyo.[7]

Restoration of the Organization and the Doctrine

On February 16, 1906, just after his return from Japan, the *Sŏngsa* had proclaimed a Ch'ŏndogyo constitution which included in its provisions the regular observance of Sunday as *siil* (rest day) and the regular conduct of religious services. These services were to be centered around the following traditional Ch'ŏndogyo observances:

1. Performance of *chumun* (ritual, based upon the Sacred Formula of Ch'ŏndogyo).

2. The administering of *ch'ŏngsu* (pure water) as an act of religious symbolism analogous to baptism.

3. The presentation of *sŏngmi* (sincerity rice) as a contribution to the self-support of the Ch'ŏndogyo sect.

4. The observance of *kido* (prayer).[8]

In 1907, Son Pyŏng-hi, the *Sŏngsa,* embarked on an extensive campaign of evangelization and recruitment throughout northwestern, northeastern, and southern Korea, and made progress in rebuilding the membership of Ch'ŏndogyo. In the same year, he organized for the first time a *Kyori Kangsŭpso* (Religious Training Institute) in Seoul to train young men in Ch'ŏndogyo doctrine. Similar institutes were later set up in various districts throughout the country. In 1909, he established Tongdŏk Girls' High School, and in 1910, Posŏng College, Posŏng Boys' High School, Posŏng Primary School, and a teachers' training school. Also in 1910, Son began publication of a monthly magazine.

In January, 1911, the *Sŏngsa* formulated and put into effect a second constitution which created two new administrative organs: (1) a central office of inspection and control, called *Taejongsa;* and (2) an office in charge of all spiritual affairs, known as the *Tosasil* (Office of Affairs of the Way).[9]

In April, 1911, the *Sŏngsa* took still another step in his campaign to revitalize Ch'ŏndogyo by establishing in Seoul a second *Kyori Kangsŭpso* (Religious Training Institute). At this institute, instruction was given not only to young recruits but also to 500 key Ch'ŏndogyo leaders selected from local districts. All the students were taught the observance of the traditional Ch'ŏndogyo ritual and of forty-nine days' prayer. In addition, they were instructed along the following lines on basic and applied Ch'ŏndogyo doctrine:

1. *In Nae Ch'ŏn* (Man and God are One). Son Pyŏng-hi, the *Sŏngsa,* felt that, although most followers of the Way had an appreciation for the spirit of the *Taesinsa* (the Great Divine Teacher, Ch'oe Che-u), many of them had not

[7]*Ch'ŏndogyo Ch'ang Kŏn Sa,* Pt. II, pp. 55-61; also Clark, *op. cit.,* pp. 151-153.

[8]*Ch'ŏndogyo Ch'ang Kŏn Sa,* Pt. III, p. 54.   [9]*Ibid.,* pp. 62-64.

fully grasped the meaning of *in nae ch'ŏn,* the basic religious principle of Ch'ŏndogyo (see Chapter II, above).

2. *Sŏngsin Ssangjŏn* (Unity of Mind and Matter). The *Sŏngsa* developed this idea as an explanation of the *Taesinsa's* three principles of *poguk anmin* (welfare of the country and safety for the people); *p'odŏk ch'ŏnha* (propagation of the faith throughout the world); and *kwangje ch'angsaeng* (general equality of the people). The *Sŏngsa* reasoned that the principle of *poguk anmin* is essentially a physical matter, whereas *p'odŏk ch'ŏnha,* the most characteristic feature of Ch'ŏndogyo, concerns itself with the mind and spirit, and represents the new religious doctrine of the highest, the ultimate in religion and virtue. Basically, said the *Sŏngsa,* Ch'ŏndogyo never looks at mind and matter as two separate elements. On the contrary, believing that both mind and matter are created only through a unified spiritual motivation, Ch'ŏndogyo adheres neither to idealism nor to materialism, but concerns itself only with attaining *hanul* (Heaven), the one spiritual entity. Since mind and matter parallel each other at the point of motivation, the acceptance and carrying out of both elements are called *sŏngsin ssangjŏn* (unity of mind and matter). At the point of action, however, a distinction must be made between spiritual and physical things.

3. *Kyojŏng Ilch'i* (Consistency of Religion and Politics). The *Sŏngsa* declared that, in accordance with the principles of *in nae ch'ŏn* and *sŏngsin ssangjŏn,* moral and political matters cannot be regarded as separate from each other, from the standpoint of human relations. When these matters manifest themselves through the social or governmental *system,* they are considered to be politics. On the other hand, when they appear in the cultural field, they are regarded as being religion. Therefore, said the *Sŏngsa,* Ch'ŏndogyo considers that, in the salvation of the world, spiritual cultivation and the material system are equally important.

4. *Sŏngyŏng Ch'ulsesŏl* (Doctrine of the Transmigration of the Spirit). The *Sŏngsa* developed this concept after meditation about the lives of his predecessors, the *Taesinsa* and the *Sinsa.* The *Sŏngsa* came to feel that, although there were physical differences between the two leaders and also separations in time and space, there developed a complete unity between their spirits through participation in the same type of religious experiences. If this philosophy is developed, said the *Sŏngsa,* the energy and spirit of people from time immemorial appear in the lives of posterity for countless years in the future; that is to say, man's energy, through the transmission of his endeavors to posterity, is everlasting. The *Sŏngsa* considered this one of the most important Ch'ŏndogyo teachings.

5. *Isin Hwansŏng* (Sacrifice of the Physical for the Spiritual). This principle, said the *Sŏngsa,* means that one's life should be idealized; that man should live according to principles rather than by means of his physical body alone.

6. *Kyumo Ilch'i* (Uniformity of Discipline). From the narrow point of view, said the *Sŏngsa*, this principle means the standardization of Ch'ŏndogyo discipline. From a broader viewpoint, however, it means the same as *tong kwi il che* (all life evolves toward a social oneness). If one looks at the inequalities and irregularities of any social system with an understanding of equality and freedom and strives to harmonize these discrepancies, then Heaven will actually come on earth, declared the *Sŏngsa*.

7. *Sinang T'ongil* (Unity of Faith). The *Sŏngsa* declared that there had been, up to that time, many religions in the world with different faiths. When there is an understanding of the basic element of the Heavenly Way and all men return to the law of Nature, there will be only one faith. This, said the *Sŏngsa*, would be like the obliteration of lesser lights by the sunrise.

8. *Chonggyo ŭi Chŏngŭi* (Definition of Religion). The *Sŏngsa* declared that religion can be defined only through the development of a highly refined personality which is an integrated combination of the principles of knowledge *(chi)*, love *(chŏng)*, and will *(ŭi)*.[10]

Other Measures Taken by Son Pyŏng-hi

Son Pyŏng-hi, the *Sŏngsa*, took other steps, outside the field of reindoctrination, to put new life into his Ch'ŏndogyo movement. In 1914, he officially abolished the system of personal control of the sect and declared in favor of a division of leadership with his many followers. The *Sŏngsa* expressed his views in these words:

> From now on, Ch'ŏndogyo is destined to enjoy prosperity. There will arise again a King of Heaven, a King of Earth, and a King of Man who will be the founders of a new world. After that, a republican system of government will be established and will continue for 50,000 years. The position of *toju* (Leader of the Way) will be a type of administrative position which any member may acquire on the basis of individual virtue.[11]

In July, 1914, regional control of the reorganized Ch'ondogyo organization was strengthened by the establishment of the Religious District System *(Tae Kyoguje)*, and the resultant organization of thirty-seven districts throughout Korea.

In June, 1916, the *Sŏngsa* declared that Ch'ŏndogyo had passed the period in which members should feel the necessity to be constantly dependent upon God and the *Sŏngsa*. The time had come, he said, when each member must develop self-reliance and a sense of Heaven within himself. The principle of *in nae ch'ŏn* (Man and God are one), continued the *Sŏngsa*, will never change, but religious *systems* will change. He said that there will be "small changes within ten years, moderate changes in 100 years, and great changes in 1,000 years."[12] In other words, Ch'ŏndogyo members, while conducting their lives in accordance with the immutable principle of *in nae ch'ŏn*, must prepare themselves to assume their proper roles of leadership under evolving conditions.

---

[10]*Ibid.*, pp. 66-69.   [11]*Ibid.*, p. 70.   [12]*Ibid.*, pp. 71-72.

Growing Korean Sentiment for Independence
While the *Sŏngsa* was revitalizing Ch'ŏndogyo, the Japanese government
General, under General Terauchi from 1910 to 1916 and Hasegawa from
1916 to 1919, was employing the most extreme police state methods in governing Korea. The civil and military police carried out administrative and judicial
functions as well as police duties. Through the police, moreover, Japanese
officials at the local, county, and provincial levels maintained constant, close
observation and control of every important aspect of the personal life of the
Koreans. With a highly regimented educational system as a base, the Japanese
regime attempted to wipe out the Koreans' national consciousness and the
distinctly Korean cultural institutions.[13]

Though the Japanese regime brought extensive material improvements in
agriculture, industry, and public utilities, these changes were directed toward
building up the economy of Japan rather than that of Korea. Deliberate Japanese exploitation of the Koreans took place in many economic areas. Probably
the most bitterly resented of these measures was the virtual confiscation of the
best Korean farm lands, through the employment of economic pressures and
intimidation through the government-controlled Oriental Development Company, established in 1907.[14]

During the five years of the protectorate, and even for a time after the annexation in 1910, a significant number of patriotic Koreans had accepted the
coming of Japanese rule as an unavoidable, temporary evil, or even as a desirable harbinger of just and enlightened government for Korea. However, as a
result of the extreme harshness and inflexibility of the Japanese colonial administration, these optimists were disillusioned and the Korean people as a
whole became increasingly restive. This nation-wide reaction against Japanese rule during the nine years of the Terauchi and Hasegawa regimes was a
major factor in the development of a new, purposeful, broad-based Korean
national spirit.[15]

An important training ground for nationalist leaders was a nationalist-
independence organization known as the *Sinmin Hoe* (New People's Society).
This society, organized during the preannexation period by the Christian,
Western-educated leader An Ch'ang-ho, operated effectively until 1913. The
Sinmin Hoe concealed its secret nationalist character through the operation of
a network of schools, bookstores, and industrial plants. The Japanese author-

[13]Pak Un-sik, *Han'guk Tongnip Undong Chi Hyŏlsa* [The Bloody History of the Korean Independence Move-
ment] (Shanghai, Yusinsa, 1920), Pt. I, pp. 32-59.

[14]*Ibid.;* also C. Clyde Mitchell, *Final Report and History of the New Korea Company,* Hq. U. S. Army Military
Govt. In Korea, 1948, pp. 2-4; C. Martin Wilbur, "Japan and the Korean Farmer," *Asia,* Vol. XXXV, No. 6 (June,
1935), pp. 394-397.

[15]Japanese Govt. General in Korea, *Chŏsen no Dokuritsu Shisŏ Oyobi Undŏ* [Korean Independence Thought and
Activities] (Seoul, 1924), pp. 2-37. This study, originally secret, attempts to analyze Korean resentments against the
Japanese. See also Pak Un-sik, *op. cit.,* Pt. II, pp. 91-100.

ities became increasingly suspicious, but were never able to gain evidence of criminal activity against any of the specific *Sinmin Hoe* enterprises. Apparently in order to get at the organization and its principal leaders, the Japanese authorities manufactured a "conspiracy" to assassinate Governor General Terauchi. The "conspiracy trials" of 1912-1913 were an utter travesty of justice. The Japanese authorities were unable to produce any evidential basis for conviction on the charges, but nevertheless imprisoned most of the principal *Sinmin Hoe* leaders. The trials thus marked the end of the society's organized existence, but also had the effect of stirring further popular resentment against the Japanese. Many of the *Sinmin Hoe* leaders involved in the "Conspiracy Case" later assumed positions of leadership in the national anti-Japanese uprising of 1919.[16]

The emergence of spiritually and organizationally strong religious groups was a major factor in the effective mobilization of the new Korean national spirit.

Ch'ŏndogyo, through the *Sŏngsa*'s intensive revitalization program, was transformed from a weak, loosely organized society associated with the Japanese-sponsored program of "reforms" into a well-disciplined, well-indoctrinated patriotic cult. By March, 1919, the movement had built up a large, nation-wide membership.[17] While confining its activities primarily to those of a religious group, Ch'ŏndogyo was qualifying itself to assume a leading role in the cause of Korean nationalism and independence. Its qualifications for such leadership were strengthened by the fact that the *Sŏngsa* had been able to accomplish his remarkable transformation of the movement without arousing the opposition of the Japanese authorities, who apparently still considered him pro-Japanese.[18]

The Protestant Christian groups — principally Presbyterians and Methodists — also developed into a strong, militant force during the pre-1919 period. The Western missionaries who had established and guided these Protestant sects in Korea had contributed significantly to this strengthening process by laying constant stress on the development of local self-support and administrative autonomy. The Korean Protestants continued to rely on their Western mentors for substantial material support and guidance, however, and maintained close contacts with them. Through these associations, the Korean Protestant Christians acquired considerable knowledge and understanding of the spiritual values of Western democracy. At the same time, they became peculiarly aware of the extent to which economic, social, and political rights taken for granted in

[16]Kim Tŭk-hwang, *Han'guk Sasang Sa* [History of Korean Thought] (Seoul: Namsandang, 1958), pp. 267-269; also Aeguk Tongji Wŏnhohoe [Relief Society for Patriotic Compatriots], *Han'guk Tongnip Undong Sa* [History of the Korean Independence Movement] (Seoul, 1956), p. 91.

[17]Ch'ŏndogyo claimed between 1,500,000 and 2,000,000 by 1919, and qualified Western observers in Korea at that time were inclined to credit them with a membership of perhaps 1,000,000. Clark, *op. cit.*, p. 169; Henry Chung, *The Case of Korea* (New York, Revell, 1921) p. 198; McKenzie, *op. cit.*, pp. 241-242.

[18]Chung, *op. cit.*, p. 198; McKenzie, *op. cit.*, pp. 241-242; Hulbert, "Religion of the Heavenly Way," *Korea Review*, Nov. 1906, p. 424.

the West were being trampled upon and stamped out by the Japanese police. Moreover, the Korean Protestants found a close parallel to contemporary Korean experiences in the Biblical accounts of the trials of the children of Israel under foreign bondage. As the pressures of Japanese domination became increasingly intense, these Korean Christians identified the Korean people as the enslaved Israelites and the Japanese as the foreign oppressors. To the Christians, similarly, the Korean independence leaders were counterparts of Moses, and the entire Korean nationalist upsurge acquired a Scriptural endorsement.[19]

The Korean Catholic Christians were, as individuals, as interested as any patriotic Koreans in ridding their nation of foreign tyranny. As has been seen in Chapter I, above, the early Catholic Christians in Korea had undergone severe, recurrent persecutions for their faith at the hands of the tyrannical Korean rulers of the eighteenth and nineteenth centuries. As a result of the long suppression by the government, however, the Korean Catholics had been unable to develop strong leadership. For this reason, and apparently also for reasons of Church policy at the time, the Korean Catholics, as such, did not participate prominently in nationalist activities during the Japanese regime.[20]

Korean Buddhism developed new strength during the 1910-1919 period. Buddhist temples and monks had been banned from Korean cities during most of the Yi Dynasty down to the establishment of the Japanese Protectorate in 1905. Although many individual Koreans had continued to adhere to Buddhist ritualistic practices and to support the monasteries, Buddhism was officially regarded as degrading until 1905. Ironically, it was the Japanese policy of strengthening sects also active in Japan which enabled the Korean Buddhists to rebuild their organization during the 1910-1919 period. The principal Korean Buddhist leaders, however, resisted Japanese pressures to use their sect as an instrument of Japanese policy, and showed themselves to be patriotic Koreans. The Buddhists were therefore in a position, by 1919, to provide some active support for a nation-wide nationalist-independence program.[21]

While the leaders and organizations in Korea were reacting quietly but positively to the pressures of the Japanese colonial regime, groups of Korean exiled nationalist leaders were working to advance Korea's cause from several foreign vantage points. The principal foreign centers were the continental United States and Hawaii; Shanghai, China; and maritime Siberia and southern Manchuria, just across Korea's northern borders. The exiled leaders, through reasonably effective communications with their colleagues inside

[19]Cynn, Hugh Houng-wo, *The Rebirth of Korea* (New York: Abingdon Press, 1920), pp. 126-148; also Alfred W. Wasson, *Church Growth in Korea* (New York: International Missionary Council, 1934), pp. 78-102.

[20]Sin T'ae-ak, "Samil Undong ŭi Chudong Immul ŭn Nugu" [Who Was the Principal Individual in the March First Movement?], *Hanguk Ilbo* [Korea Daily News], July 10, 1957, p. 4.

[21]Pak Un-sik, *op. cit.*, Pt. II, pp. 97-99.

Korea, kept abreast of developments there and also helped to built up a conviction within Korea that World War I, then in progress, was a righteous crusade against tyranny—in Korea as elsewhere.[22]

Within Korea, the Protestant Christian groups, because of their associations with missionaries and other contacts with the West, were a major channel for spreading the idealistic hope that an Allied victory would bring an end to the foreign domination of small nations, including Korea. In fact, since Japan was fighting on the side of the Allies, even the Japanese-controlled press in Korea covered war developments in such a way as to encourage such sentiment among the Koreans.[23]

The principal spark to these Korean liberation hopes came from the Wilsonian philosophy of "self-determination of peoples" and the efforts of the delegates to the Paris Peace Conference to establish a new, equitable world order. These announced aims seemed to Korean nationalist leaders, both in Korea and abroad, to offer them their long-sought hope of freedom and independence.[24]

Various groups among the nationalist intellectuals within and outside Korea began thinking about some anti-Japanese demonstration at roughly the same time. In Korea and Japan, student groups also reacted and began making plans for a demonstration. However, the actual uprising in March, 1919, was a unified one, participated in by all nationalist elements, and headed up by Son Pyŏng-hi, the *Sŏngsa*.[25]

Organization and planning work for the independence uprising began to take shape before the end of hostilities in Europe. In October, 1918, an independence movement headquarters was set up in Seoul, as a direct result Nam-sŏn, Song Chin-u, Ch'oe Rin, and Hyŏn Sang-yun. The latter two were prominent Ch'ŏndogyo members.

The planners agreed from the outset that the uprising would be a unified, nonviolent, nation-wide demonstration to the world of the determination of the Korean people to be free. They asked former Yi Dynasty officials, Christian leaders, Buddhist abbots, and other representative Korean elements to participate in the movement. The three groups which actually furnished the principal leadership for the entire movement were: Ch'ŏndogyo, the Protestant Churches, and the Buddhist abbots. The representatives on the Preparatory Committee in the headquarters in Seoul were: for Ch'ŏndogyo—Son Pyŏng-hi, Kwŏn Tong-jin, and O Se-ch'ang; for the Christians—Yi Sung-hun,

---

[22]Kim Tŭk-hwang, *op. cit.*, pp. 267-269.

[23]Cynn, *op. cit.*, pp. 16-17; Wasson, *op. cit.*, p. 98. Also Japanese Military Police Headquarters in Korea, *Taishō Hachinen Chōsen Shōyō Jiken Jōkyō* [A Report on the Korean Disturbance of 1919], pp. 181 f. This official report of Japanese police investigations (originally secret) gives a very thorough, generally factual account of preparations for the independence uprising. The report stresses the close associations of missionaries and Korean Christians.

[24]Pak Un-sik, *op.cit.*, Pt. II. p. 6. Chung, *op.cit.*, pp. 191-192; McKenzie, *op.cit.*, p. 243.

[25]Pak Un-sik, *op. cit.*, Pt. II, p. 6. Also, Kim Sang-dŏk *Chosŏn Tongnip Undong Sa* [History of the Korean Independence Movement] (Seoul: Chosŏn Publication and Culture Co., 1946), pp. 11-14.

Pak Hi-do, and Ham T'ae-yŏng; and for the Buddhists—Han Yong-un and Paek Yong-sŏng. Son Pyŏng-hi was chosen chairman of the headquarters group and thus became the principal leader of the uprising.

At a first series of conferences in the fall of 1918, the top leaders organized the national headquarters and agreed on plans for branch offices in all of the thirteen provinces.[26]

In the course of the preparatory conferences, the representatives of all participating groups assumed the responsibility for organizing the movement among their own constituents, in close coordination with the national headquarters. Each group also assumed certain specific responsibilities. The Christians, for example, accepted the task of preparing documents to be presented to the President of the United States (President Wilson) and the Paris Peace Conference. Ch'ŏndogyo utilized its organizational facilities and managerial experience in the interests of the movement as a whole. For example, funds from the Ch'ŏndogyo treasury were made available for the use of the Christian participants in the demonstration, and also for the activities of Korean representatives abroad. In addition, the Ch'ŏndogyo organization printed large numbers of pamphlets and posters for distribution throughout the country, and lithographed, from hand-carved woodblocks, the Korean declaration of independence and a memorandum to the Japanese Government.[27]

During the early stages of preparations, the leaders in Seoul made preliminary contact with Korean students in Japan, with a view to bringing them into the final planning for a demonstration. As a result, a group of some five hundred Korean students gathered in Tokyo on December 28-29, 1918, and held an extended discussion on self-government. The Japanese police arrested a few of the students but, apparently considering the incident an isolated one, released them within a few days. The group in Japan later sent representatives to Seoul to confer with the top leaders there on the later phases of the planning.[28]

Early in 1919, leading students in Seoul boarding schools, who would normally have been home for the winter vacation, remained in the city to take part in planning anti-Japanese action. At about the same time, delegates from the Korean communities in Shanghai and across the northern Korean borders began to slip into Seoul and establish communications between their groups and the Seoul headquarters. One of the representatives from Shanghai was charged with obtaining funds from Ch'ŏndogyo for the expenses of Korean emissaries to the Peace Conference at Paris and to other world centers.[29]

---

[26]Pak Un-sik, *op. cit.*, Pt. II, pp. 6-7; Japanese Govt. General in Korea, *Korean Independence Thought and Activities*, pp. 38-80.

[27]Cho Chong-o, *Chosŏn Ch'aegŭn Samdae Undongsa* [A History of The Three Largest Movements in Korea in Recent Times] (Seoul: Unghyŏn Kurakpu Ch'ul P'anbu, 1946), pp. 40-43; Kim Sang-dŏk, *op. cit.*, p. 12.

[28]Aeguk Tongji Wŏnhohoe, *op. cit.*, pp. 410-420.

[29]Cho Chong-o, *op. cit.*, pp. 40-43; Kim Sang-dŏk, *op. cit.*, pp. 11 f.

The former Emperor Kwang-mu, who had been deposed by the Japanese in 1907 in favor of his son, died suddenly on January 22, 1919. It is strongly believed by Korean historians and Koreans generally that the Emperor was poisoned by the Japanese because he had refused to sign a petition to the Paris Peace Conference to the effect that Japan and Korea should remain united because of close cultural ties.

The Emperor's death and the widespread conviction that he had been murdered by the Japanese added a powerful emotional fervor to the already highly charged atmosphere in Seoul and in the foreign centers of Korean nationalist activity.

In Korea, school children stayed home from school, theatres were empty, the traditional festivities of the lunar New Year season were suspended, and most of the people put on their grass-cloth mourning robes.

In Japan, a second gathering of Korean students took place on February 8, at which the principal speaker spoke with great emotion about the death of the former Emperor, the colonial slavery of the Korean people, and the opportunity presented to the Koreans by the coming peace conference in Paris. He climaxed his call for action by pricking his finger and writing in blood a petition to the Japanese Parliament asking for Korean independence. After all of the six hundred present had signed the petition, the Japanese police broke up the meeting and arrested some sixty of the boys.[30]

During February, the Preparatory Committee and component elements of the movement reached the final stages of their preparations. The final details and timing apparently were not decided until the latter part of February. The date was set for March 1, to take advantage of the anticipated presence in Seoul of hundreds of thousands of people for the funeral of the former Emperor. The Declaration of Independence, written by Ch'oe Nam-sŏn, would be signed by ten or more representatives each of Ch'ŏndogyo and the Protestant Christians, as well as an indefinite number of Buddhist representatives.[31]

The Declaration would be formally proclaimed at 2:00 P.M. on the first, when Son Pyŏng-hi would read it in the presence of the other signers, at a public place in the heart of Seoul. This would be followed by the launching of simultaneous local demonstrations throughout the country and the distribution of large numbers of pamphlets and posters which had previously been prepared and delivered to central points.[32]

The March 1 demonstration was carried out precisely as planned. All the detailed, secret planning described above was conducted without detection by the

---

[30]Aeguk Tongji Wŏnhohoe, *op. cit.,* pp. 410-420.

[31]Aoyagi Nammei, *Chōsen Dokuritsu Shōyō Shiron* [An Historical Account of Korea's Independence Disturbance] (Seoul: Korea Statistical Assn., 1921), Appendix, pp. 347-427. This appendix contains the record of the trials of the independence uprising.

[32]*Ibid;* also Japanese Govt. General in Korea, *Korean Independence Thought and Activities,* pp. 66-67.

numerous, ever-present Japanese police. On the appointed day, March 1, Son Pyŏng-hi and the thirty-two other signers of the Declaration of Independence dined together at a well-known restaurant at Pagoda Park in the center of Seoul. At the appointed hour, 2 P.M., they drank a toast to Korean freedom and independence, read the Declaration of Independence, and raised independence cheers. They then sent a complimentary copy of the Declaration to the Japanese Governor-General and telephoned the Central Police Station, reporting their actions and stating that they were awaiting arrest. The signers were promptly picked up in a police wagon and driven off to the Police Station through streets packed with wildly cheering crowds.[33]

This was the dramatic signal which set off simultaneous demonstrations elsewhere in Seoul and throughout the country. It soon became apparent that the uprising was truly a national one, in which diverse Korean religious, economic, and social elements — men, women, and children — were united as they had not been united for centuries.[34]

Students played an important part in the activities. In Seoul, five or six thousand student representatives participated in the initial demonstration at Pagoda Park, and many others demonstrated and marched throughout the city, visiting such points as the French and American Consulates, the Government-General building, and even the Japanese Army barracks where they tried unsuccessfully to obtain arms. A total of 130 students were arrested in Seoul on March 1.[35]

Son Pyŏng-hi, the *Sŏngsa,* and hundreds of other leaders in the independence uprising were imprisoned, and many of the peaceful demonstrators, all unarmed and unresisting, were tortured or killed in the ruthless suppression by the Japanese authorities.

The new Korean spirit of indomitable espousal of the cause of nationalism and independence is graphically described in the following passage:

. . . The Korean's love of country has been learned in the losing of it, and the value of liberty in the deprivation of it. The process of denationalization, forced upon Korea by Japan, served as a crucible in which Korean patriotism was crystalized. During the fifteen years of tyrannical domination, Japan, unconsciously, and in spite of herself, gave Korea a new hope, an ideal and a fighting spirit. Now Korea is no longer the Korea of traditional sloth. A fresh impulse has been generated throughout Korea, and the awakening of a vital nationalism has taken place. The people have become conscious of the meaning of their nationhood, and are sacrificing themselves for the realization of it. They have opened their eyes to the world outside their peninsula and are eager to fall in with its step. No longer can the soldier's rifle or the gendarme's sword cow them. This is the spirit which brought about the Independence Movement of 1919.[36]

---

[33]Chung, *op. cit.,* pp. 204-205; McKenzie, *op. cit.,* pp. 246-250. The 33 signers were: 15 Ch'ŏndogyo leaders; 16 Protestant Christian representatives (including four from the YMCA and one student from the Christian medical college); and two Buddhist priests. O Chae-sik, *Hang-Il Sun'guk Uiyŏ sa Chŏn* [Biography of Martyred Anti-Japanese Patriots] (Seoul: Aeguk Chŏngsin Sonyanghoe, 1957), p. 100.

[34]McKenzie, *op. cit.,* p. 252.   [35]Kim Sang-dŏk, *op. cit.,* pp. 11-14.

[36]Chung, *op. cit.,* pp. 191-192; see also Aoyagi Nammei, *op. cit.,* p. 417; McKenzie, *op. cit.,* pp. 251-261.

The conduct of the Korean victims in the face of brutal Japanese police measures did as much to kindle a lasting flame of Korean nationalism and to awaken world opinion against Japanese colonial methods as did the demonstration itself. Documents condemning Japanese methods in Korea and urging diplomatic action by the United States government to effect Korean independence were presented to Congress and published in the Congressional Record. These included statements by a former U.S. Minister to Korea (Dr. H. N. Allen) and a former confidential advisor to the Korean Emperor (Prof. Homer B. Hulbert); a report by the Federal Council of the Churches of Christ in America; a resolution of a mass meeting of citizens of Philadelphia; and a formal statement and brief for the Republic of Korea. Resolutions expressing sympathy with the aspirations of the Korean people for a government of their own choice were introduced in both the Senate and the House of Representatives during the 66th Congress (October, 1919), and the House Resolution was reintroduced in the 67th Congress (April, 1921). None of these resolutions reached the floor of Congress for action, presumably because American sympathy for Korea, though strong, was not sufficiently powerful to impel Congress to attempt to oppose the current U.S. foreign policy for the Far East which envisaged continued friendly relations with Japan.[37] A request in the British House of Commons for a government report on Japanese treatment of Korean Christians involved in the March, 1919, uprising indicates that there was some popular reaction in Great Britain to Korean developments. No official British action in favor of Korea could have been expected, since the Anglo-Japanese alliance was still in force.[38]

The Korean Provisional Government and the Independence Movement Outside Korea After March, 1919

One of the concrete results of the Korean national awakening which accompanied the March, 1919 movement was the establishment of the Korean Provisional Government which operated in exile in China until the Japanese surrender in 1945. To the outside world, this provisional government in exile was the embodiment of the Korean national spirit and of Korean aspirations for independence.

The draft constitution was prepared and the first cabinet (headed by Dr. Syngman Rhee) was selected by a generally representative body of Korean nationalists from all the thirteen Korean provinces, in a secret meeting in Seoul early in April, 1919.[39] Messengers from Independence headquarters in Seoul went to Shanghai and directed the established independence group there to set up the Korean Provisional Government headquarters. The emissaries also

[37]*Congressional Record, 66th Congress, 1st Session,* pp. 2594, 2597, 2697, 3924, 5595, 6611, 6813, 6817, 6818, and 6822; *Ibid., 2nd Session,* p. 8160; *Congressional Record, 68th Congress, 1st Session,* p. 101; *Ibid., 2nd Session,* pp. 344, 1747, 3057, 4183, and 10072.

[38]Hansard, *Parliamentary Debates,* Vol. 117 (1919), p. 1393.

[39]McKenzie, *op. cit.,* pp. 303-308.

delivered to the group the list of Cabinet ministers and a copy of the draft constitution.[40]

Importance of Son Pyŏng-hi's Leadership, 1906-1922

From the beginning of the Japanese protectorate in 1906 until Son Pyŏng-hi's death in 1922, the outstanding feature of the Ch'ŏndogyo movement was the towering figure of Son, the *Sŏngsa*. His zeal, administrative skill, and political astuteness almost completely molded and dominated the movement. When, at the beginning of this period, Son's policies and position of leadership were challenged by the pro-Japanese Yi Yong-gu, Son succeeded in purging the dissident elements and remolding the movement in accordance with traditional Tonghak concepts of its proper religio-nationalist role.

Under Son's leadership during the 1906-1922 period, Ch'ŏndogyo maintained its underlying ethical and social objectives: the realization of the principles of *sa in yŏ ch'ŏn* (treat people as though they were God) and *tong kwi il ch'e* (all life evolves toward a social oneness), in a society motivated by the basic concept of *in nae ch'ŏn* (Man and God are one). The political objectives also remained partially constant, inasmuch as they continued to include the achievement of fundamental domestic reforms. However, with the progressive solidification of Japanese control, the overriding political objective of Ch'ŏndogyo under Son Pyŏng-hi's leadership became the reestablishment of Korean independence.

If, however, the *Sŏngsa* was to perfect or implement any program for the achievement of these objectives, or indeed if Ch'ŏndogyo was to survive as a genuine Korean nationalist movement, prompt, drastic action to dissociate the organization from all pro-Japanese activity was obviously imperative. In the face of persistent pro-Japanese actions on the part of Yi Yong-gu and his faction, therefore, Son Pyŏng-hi had no alternative but to resort to a purge, despite the obvious risks involved. The thorough and successful manner in which the purge was accomplished is more significant than the fact of the purge itself. The *Sŏngsa's* purge of his organization was so deep that it encompassed virtually all of the experienced leaders and deprived the organization of all its corporate property; but these serious handicaps were overcome by Son's energetic program of rebuilding and revitalization.

Son Pyŏng-hi, the *Sŏngsa*, had a clear understanding of the fundamental importance of doctrine and ritual in the development and maintenance of strength and *esprit de corps* within Ch'ŏndogyo. This was demonstrated initially when, immediately upon his return from Japan, he instituted regular observance of Sunday as a rest day and reinstituted regular worship centering about traditional Ch'ŏndogyo rituals and observances. This utilization of doctrine and ritual was intensified and systematized by means of the extensive educational system established by the *Sŏngsa*, notably the Religious Training

---

[40]Pak, *op. cit.*, p. 56.

Institutes for actual and prospective Ch'ŏndogyo leaders. The subject matter covered in this indoctrination was generally theoretical, consisting of an intensive review and reinterpretation of the Ch'ŏndogyo philosophy inspired by Ch'oe Che-u, the *Taesinsa*. It seems reasonable to conclude that the content of such a heavy course of study was largely lost on the majority of the students. Subsequent events appear to be adequate proof, however, of the success of this indoctrination effort in instilling a new *esprit de corps* among the leaders of the movement.

The *Sŏngsa* also demonstrated his ability to strengthen the movement through adopting flexible administrative policies. Central control of the organization had been relatively loose during the Tonghak period when strong local units (*p'o*) were the mainstay of the movement. The local units continued to be basic, but the conditions confronting Son and his organization during this period of rehabilitation after 1906 dictated the superimposition of new regional administrative units to strengthen control from central headquarters and to foster an increased sense of unity among the members. It is clear that the *Sŏngsa* was not interested in centralized power as such, since he simultaneously placed new stress on the importance of individual initiative and the selection of leaders on the basis of individual virtue.

Techniques Employed During the 1906-1922 Period

In view of the continuing leadership of Son Pyŏng-hi after Japanese control was established in Korea, it is only logical and natural that previously employed techniques would continue in use during the remainder of his period of leadership, so far as they remained feasible and effective. The four major techniques which had been employed during the Tonghak period were: (1) passive reform; (2) petitioning the government; (3) armed rebellion; and (4) collaboration with a foreign power (Japan).

As has been seen, the passive reform techniques of the Tonghak period were utilized and strengthened by Son Pyŏng-hi in his successful campaign to rehabilitate and redirect the Ch'ŏndogyo movement. He placed particular stress upon the passive reform technique of developing a nucleus of devoted, indoctrinated followers to spread the doctrine and to assume key positions of leadership.

With the government of Korea in the hands of a foreign power, the traditional practice of petitioning the government, formerly used by Ch'ŏndogyo, was no longer expedient as a standard technique. It was, however, used as a subsidiary device in the new technique of nonviolent rebellion employed in March, 1919.

During the Japanese period, armed rebellion was not used, partly because Japanese police controls made the acquisition of arms virtually impossible, partly because this technique had failed in the Tonghak period, and partly because of a desire to avoid adverse world opinion. Western language writers have generally given the Christian leaders full credit for the peaceful character of the 1919 uprising. The Korean and Japanese sources indicate, however, that Son Pyŏng-hi and the other responsible Ch'ŏndogyo leaders were equally in favor of peaceful means.

Collaboration with Japan during the Japanese control period would obviously have been incompatible with Son Pyŏng-hi's nationalistic objectives.

The New Technique of Nonviolent Rebellion

The Ch'ŏndogyo leaders had been waiting for an opportunity to lead some sort of anti-Japanese uprising. One important reason was a desire to redeem the Ch'ŏndogyo record of collaboration with the Japanese during and following the Russo-Japanese War.[41] As has been noted, there were, by early in 1919, ample motivations for some type of mass demonstration against Japanese control of Korea. The timing was designed to capitalize on world opinion at the time of the Paris Peace Conference in the hope that resultant moral forces in Korea's favor might be strong enough to bring about Korean independence. This type of aim was not to be achieved by force of arms, even if weapons had been available. Nor could the purpose be accomplished by any local or disorganized action. The Ch'ŏndogyo leaders and others associated with them came to realize that the demonstration, to be effective, must be dramatic, and that to be dramatic it must be nation-wide, enjoy spontaneous mass support, and be carefully planned. The conditions of the times, therefore, all but dictated the employment of the technique of nonviolent rebellion.

The fact that the 1919 uprising was *unified* and *nation-wide* is its most noteworthy feature, in terms of Ch'ŏndogyo techniques. As has been seen, Ch'ŏndogyo activities in the Tonghak period had been entirely sectarian in character, with the single exception of the ill-fated association with pro-Japanese reform elements in the *Ilchin Hoe* during and immediately following the Russo-Japanese War. Also, although the Ch'ŏndogyo movement had gradually spread throughout Korea, its activities prior to the period of Japanese control had been largely concentrated in the southern provinces. The decision to conduct one cooperative, nation-wide effort in 1919 was probably prompted both by the lack of complete success of earlier separate activities and by the new Korean national consciousness which had been catalyzed largely by the harsh Japanese colonial administration.

The fact that virtually all of the active leaders of the uprising were either Ch'ŏndogyo members or Protestant Christians is noteworthy. The Ch'ŏndogyo organizers, whose own movement had a strong organizational structure but a relatively small group of intellectual leaders and no significant contacts abroad, felt the need of support from groups which had intellectual leadership, organizational ability and experience, and also international contacts. In 1919, the Protestant Christians were the only group which satisfied these requirements.[42]

---

[41]Sin T'ae-ak, *op. cit.*, p. 4.   [42]*Ibid.*

The achievement of surprise despite the extensive, meticulous planning required for the nonviolent uprising furnishes proof of the shrewdness and dedication of the Ch'ŏndogyo planners and their associates. Although the Japanese authorities apparently were generally aware that something was in the air, they did not learn enough about the nature of the plan or the identity of the leaders to take preventive action. One key defection would have been sufficient to destroy the entire plan, and the defector would probably have been generously rewarded by the Japanese.

The success of the planning stage of the uprising was due in very large measure to: (1) the ability and experience of the Ch'ŏndogyo leaders and their Christian associates; (2) the efficient organizational structure of the Ch'ŏndogyo movement; and (3) the financial resources made available through Ch'ŏndogyo's *Sŏngmi* (Sincerity Rice) Fund. The long experience of Son Pyŏng-hi and his Ch'ŏndogyo subordinates with the Japanese had taught them how to operate without arousing Japanese suspicions. The stratified Ch'ŏndogyo organization, from national headquarters to local unit *(p'o)* through regional and district offices, was ideally suited to the purpose of passing secret instructions throughout the country efficiently and safely. The Sŏngmi Fund, built up through the regular contributions of Ch'ŏndogyo members at the rate of a spoonful of rice per day, furnished financial support for all nationalist elements participating with Ch'ŏndogyo in the uprising.

The nonviolent rebellion technique utilized in the demonstration of 1919 did not achieve the ultimate objective of regaining Korean independence.[43] It did, however, succeed in acquainting the world with the national aspirations of the Korean people and with the ruthless Japanese administration in Korea. The world reaction, though not such as to bring foreign pressure upon Japan for the granting of Korean independence, did impel the Japanese government to institute, for some ten years, a less harsh and superficially benevolent administration by the Government General in Korea. The most lasting result of the nonviolent rebellion of 1919, however, was the emergence of a deep, vigorous, united Korean national spirit. March 1, 1919, is still celebrated by Koreans of all religious and political creeds as the birth date of Korean independence.

Although the motivation for the 1919 uprising had come from within Korea, it was strongly encouraged and assisted by Koreans abroad. Of the various Korean nationalist groups outside Korea prior to the uprising, the one which had the closest contacts with the headquarters group in Seoul was the nucleus of independence leaders in Shanghai. The leaders in Seoul dispatched to Shanghai representatives with documents and instructions. When the Shanghai group needed financial assistance, it sent a messenger to the Seoul headquarters. The Shanghai unit had most of its direct dealings in Korea with the

---

[43]Stephen Bonsal, *Suitors and Suppliants* (New York: Prentice-Hall, 1946), pp. 222-226. Bonsal gives an account of the failure of the Korean delegate, Kimm Kiusic, to secure a hearing of the Korean case at the Paris Peace Conference, because of Japan's position as one of the victorious Allies.

Ch'ŏndogyo leaders, because: (1) Ch'ŏndogyo had money with no foreign strings attached, whereas the Christian organizations received funds from abroad; (2) Ch'ŏndogyo was, in other respects as well, completely indigenous; and (3) the Ch'ŏndogyo people were less suppressed by the Japanese authorities than were the Christians.

For these reasons, and for the additional reason that few Ch'ŏndogyo people had the necessary foreign contacts to enable them to go abroad for study or business, Ch'ŏndogyo independence activities continued to be confined largely to Korea. However, some Ch'ŏndogyo members participated, with Christians and other elements, in the Korean Provisional Government, which was established in Shanghai as a result of the 1919 nonviolent rebellion.[44]

---

[44]Sin T'ae-ak, "Samil Undong ŭi Chudong Inmul ŭn Nugu," *op. cit.*, p. 4.

The Central Cathedral of Ch'ŏndogyo in Seoul

(Official Ch'ŏndogyo photograph)

CHAPTER VII
THE HEAVENLY WAY GOES UNDERGROUND

Changes in Leadership and Administration

The active leadership of Son Pyŏng-hi, the *Sŏngsa,* ended with his arrest on March 1, 1919, but he continued to make his great influence felt from his prison cell until he died on May 19, 1922. While in prison, Son had designated as his successor Pak In-ho, one of his principal subordinates. Within two weeks after the *Sŏngsa*'s death, however, Pak In-ho, apparently sensing an undercurrent of controversy over the future leadership of the cult, submitted his resignation to a convention of Ch'ŏndogyo leaders. The convention did not accept Pak's resignation, but decided to abolish the traditional system of unitary leadership and, on June 10, 1922, selected a forty-six member committee to decide upon the future form of organization.

The committee recommended that supreme leadership be exercised through a General Assembly *(Chongnisa Ch'onghoe),* composed of representatives from each Ch'ŏndogyo district. The General Assembly met in 1923 and acted on such minor administrative matters as: determining that the *p'o* would comprise thirty households of Ch'ŏndogyo believers; decreeing that each *p'o* should appoint a *pódŏksa* (spiritual leader); and further directing that every ten *p'o* select a *chugan pódŏksa* (principal spiritual leader). Agreement could not be reached, however, on major constitutional questions involving regulations, and the written constitution was abolished in April, 1923, in favor of an unwritten constitution.[1]

The General Assembly continued to function, however, and in April, 1925, adopted a new series of regulations concerning Ch'ŏndogyo ceremonies and forms. It was decided that Heaven Day *(Ch'ŏn Il),* Earth Day *(Chi Il),* and Man Day *(In Il)* would be observed as the three principal anniversaries of Ch'ŏndogyo, as well as the anniversaries of the birth and death of the three great Ch'ŏndogyo leaders (Ch'oe Che-u, Ch'oe Si-hyŏng, and Son Pyŏng-hi). These days were to be observed as days of prayer at home. In these regulations, the traditional Anniversary of the Master *(Toju Kinyŏm Il)* — January 16 — was abolished, despite the objection of Pak In-ho and some of his associates. In June, 1925, the General Assembly carried its action against traditional Ch'ŏndogyo forms somewhat further by preparing a new regulation providing that

---

[1]*Ch'ŏndogyo Ch'ang Kŏn Sa,* Pt. IV, pp. 1-4.

Pak In-ho, the current Ch'ŏndogyo leader (also known by the honorific *Ch'unam*) should be addressed simply as *Sŏnsaeng* (Teacher). To be sure, the regulation stipulated that he should receive the highest salary of anyone in Ch'ŏndogyo and that all important business of the sect must have his approval. In August, 1925, before the new regulation had been put into effect, the Ch'ŏndogyo clique led by O Yŏng-ch'ang objected to the proposed new regulations concerning Pak In-ho, and suggested unsuccessfully that Pak be raised in rank to that of a fourth Great Leader of the sect, on a level of equality with the first three Great Leaders. After the General Assembly's regulation was promulgated, O made his objection official by convoking his followers in Seoul and leading them in lodging a formal protest.

This controversy resulted in the division of Ch'ŏndogyo into two factions, known as the New Faction *(Sin P'a)* and the Old Faction *(Ku P'a)*. The leaders in the Central Headquarters constituted the principal strength of the New Faction, whereas those members throughout the sect who were trying to restore the old hierarchical leadership made up the Old Faction. A group called the Society to Carry Out Unification *(T'ongil Kisŏng Hoe)* was organized by Kwŏn Tong-jin in the name of conciliation between the two opposing factions, but it soon became obvious that this group was actually collaborating secretly with the Old Faction. Thereupon sixty-four principal leaders in the Central Committee proclaimed their decision to support the "orthodox" position of the New Faction. The O Yŏng-Ch'ang group (the originators of the Old Faction) and the Kwŏn Tong-jin clique (the "unification" group) — both supporting Pak In-ho as their leader — withdrew from Ch'ŏndogyo. In December, 1925, the General Assembly changed its name to Ecclesiastical Assembly *(Pŏp Hoe)*, and elected new central officers. Ch'oe Rin, who had been a key figure in planning the 1919 independence uprising, became a high official of the sect, and three years later, in December, 1928, became the new head of Ch'ŏndogyo, with the title of *Toryŏng* (Leader of the Way).[2]

Establishment of a Political Party

Six months after the beginning of the independence uprising, the Ch'ŏndogyo leadership had determined to establish a socio-political organization which would keep alive the suppressed nationalist movement within Korea. On September 2, 1919, under the leadership of Yi Ton-hwa, one of the principal subordinates of the now imprisoned *Sŏngsa*, the *Ch'ŏndogyo Ch'ŏngnyon Kyori Kang'yŏnbu* (Ch'ŏndogyo Youth Department for Study of the Doctrine) was established. The publicly announced purpose of the new organization was to propagate Ch'ŏndogyo teachings with the objective of improving Korean culture.[3] However, Ch'ŏndogyo literature published after the end of the Japanese occupation states that the actual purpose of the new unit was to provide Ch'ŏndogyo youth with improved opportunities for giving expression

---

[2]*Ibid.*, pp. 7 ff.   [3]*Ibid.*, pp. 5-7.

to the nationalistic zeal and fighting spirit which they had developed during the March 1 uprising.[4] In 1920, the name of the group was changed to *Ch'ŏndogyo Ch'ŏngnyŏn Hoe* (Ch'ŏndogyo Youth Society), and under this name it began three publications designed to improve the cultural level of various social groups and to encourage political consciousness generally. These publications were: *Sin Yŏsŏng* (New Womanhood): *Orini* (Children); and *Kaebyŏk* (Creation).[5] *Kaebyŏk*, the general organ of Ch'ŏndogyo, was devoted largely to articles on innocuous philosophical, cultural, and economic subjects which were of educational interest to Ch'ŏndogyo members, but which would not arouse the Japanese censors. Some of these articles, however, were critical of the Japanese colonial regime. For example, an editorial in the October, 1923 issue criticized an economic proposal of the Japanese Government General as follows:

It is inevitable that Korea at this present moment should maintain some connection with Japan and Koreans with Japanese. However, judging objectively, both nationalities are on different industrial bases, and to draw them closer in their business relationships would in the long run mean the industrial triumph of the nationality with a superior business power over the other. From this point of view, the decision of the Committee on the Industrial Investigation to draw Koreans and Japanese closer in their business contacts, instead of providing a special protective measure for Koreans, is after all an industrial policy only for the benefit of the Japanese.[6]

On September 2, 1923, the youth organization was reorganized once again and became a full-fledged political party under the name *Ch'ŏndogyo Chŏng'u Tang* (Ch'ŏndogyo Young Friends Party). The guiding doctrinal concepts of the new party were *chisang ch'ŏn'guk kŏnsŏl* (establishment of heaven on earth) and *sa in yŏ ch'ŏn* (treating people as though they were God). According to the official Ch'ŏndogyo history, published during the Japanese regime, a desire to realize these principles and a need for further organization because of the expansion of the Youth Society were the principal motivations for the establishment of the *Ch'ŏndogyo Chŏng'u Tang*.[7] Ch'ŏndogyo literature published since the defeat of Japan, however, points out that the new political party was needed to serve as the spearhead of political action by Ch'ŏndogyo members, as distinct from the religious activities of the Ch'ŏndogyo sect. In broader terms, the principal purpose of the party was to lead in the creation of a new Korean national spirit (or racial consciousness) and of a new society. This purpose is officially explained in the following language (published in 1947) which is at least superficially Marxian:

[4]*Ch'ŏndogyo Chŏngch'i Inyŏm*, p. 35.

[5]*Ch'ŏndogyo Ch'ang Kŏn Sa*, Pt. IV, pp. 5-7.

[6]*Kaebyŏk*, Oct. 1923, p. 61, quoted in Hongkee Karl, "A Critical Evaluation of Modern Social Trends in Korea" (Ph.D. dissertation, Dept. of Comparative Religion, University of Chicago, 1934), p. 170.

[7]*Ch'ŏndogyo Ch'ang Kŏn Sa*, Pt. IV, pp. 5-7.

Creation of Korean racial consciousness means chiefly the liberation of our people from the yoke of Japanese imperialism. Creation of Korean society means the reform of the institutions of capitalistic society and the liberation of the proletariat.[8]

At the time of formal establishment, there were 30,000 members in the party and 120 local branches throughout Korea. The organization of the party was set up on the principle of "democratic centralization." There were three levels of organization: party central headquarters *(tang ponbu)*; district branches *(chibang bu);* and local units *(chŏp)*. The *chŏp* was directly responsible to the *chibang bu,* and the *chibang bu* to the *tang ponbu.* There were two top level decision-making channels: (1) the mass meeting of the whole party; and (2) the executive structure of the party, directed by the Central Executive Committee *(Chung'ang Chip'haeng Wiwŏnhoe).* The Party Headquarters had four administrative departments under the Party Chairman: (1) General Affairs Department *(Ch'ongmu Bu)*; (2) Organization Department *(Chojik Bu):* (3) Training Department *(Hullyŏn Bu);* and (4) Propaganda Department *(Sŏnjŏn Bu).* There was also an Academic Research Department *(Haksul Yŏn'gu Bu)* which conducted studies in the fields of religion, philosophy, politics (very generalized), economics, art, sociology, and physical culture. These studies were circulated among party members and other young people, with a view to diffusing specialized knowledge and thus raising the general cultural level.

In order to develop and spread the various activities which the Party was interested in fostering, seven activity departments were established. These were: (1) Young Children's Department *(Yusonyŏn Bu)*; (2) Youth Department *(Ch'ŏngnyŏn Bu)*; (3) Student Department *(Haksaeng Bu)*; (4) Women's Department *(Yŏsŏng Bu);* (5) Farmers' Department *(Nongmin Bu);* (6) Labor Department *(Nodong Bu)*; and (7) Merchants' Department *(Sangmin Bu).* Under each of these departments, there was established a committee which studied both theories and methods as related to the problem of the department. Each of these departmental committees also recruited and trained personnel to lead the activities of each department. The activities of these departments gave rise to the following specialized agencies: (1) Children's Society *(Sonyŏn Hoe)*; (2) Youth Society *(Ch'ŏngnyŏn Hoe*; (3) Students' Society *(Haksaeng Hoe)*; (4) Korean Farmers' Institute *(Chosŏn Nongmin Sa)*; and (5) Korean Labor Institute *(Chosŏn Nodong Sa).* The Labor Institute was established only in the main cities, but the Farmers' Institute established several hundred branches on the county *(kun)* level, and claimed a total membership of several hundred thousand by the mid-1930's. As its official organs, the Farmers' Institute published *Nongmin* (The Farmer) and *Nongmin Sesang* (Farmer's World). As its economic enterprise, this institute operated farmers' cooperatives *(nongmin kongsaeng chohap),* in order to develop the farmers'

---

[8]*Ch'ŏndogyo Chŏngch'i Inyŏm*, pp. 35-37 (quot., p. 37).

immediate concern for their own livelihood in such fields as production, consumption, credit, and utilization of equipment.[9]

In 1929, the Young Friends Party, presumably for greater efficiency and greater protection from Japanese government surveillance, began conducting its operations through two secret regional subparty organizations: the *Pulbul Tang* ("Double Negative Party") with headquarters in Seoul; and the *Osim Tang* ("Our Heart Party") with headquarters in P'yŏngyang, in northern Korea. Both groups worked energetically to obtain members and funds for their nationalistic activities, and achieved considerable success for several years.[10] The *Osim Tang* seems to have been the more successful of the two groups, since, outside of the capital province of Kyŏnggi, the northern provinces of Hwanghae, South and North P'yŏngan, and South Hamgyŏng were the principal centers of party activity during this period. The *Osim Tang* established agricultural cooperatives through the Korean Farmers' Institute and issued publications designed to "develop the farmers' thoughts."[11]

After the Manchurian Incident of 1931, party activities decreased sharply in tempo, as a result of increasingly rigid Japanese surveillance and control. Apparently the last extensive effort at political activity by the Young Friends Party organization was in April, 1931, when the two branches *(Osim Tang* and *Pulbul Tang)* assembled together in Seoul for the celebration of a Ch'ŏndogyo anniversary. On this occasion, the leaders: (1) restricted membership in the party to those who had been faithful Ch'ŏndogyo members for ten years; (2) decided to take advantage of an anticipated political crisis in 1935 or 1936 to activate some sort of Korean nationalist movement; and (3) discussed plans for collecting funds for this planned movement. The leaders were all arrested by the Japanese authorities in the course of the meeting, and the plans, of course, failed.[12] Activities of the party became increasingly difficult and came virtually to a standstill in 1934, when the Japanese authorities arrested and jailed several hundred members. After the outbreak of the Sino-Japanese hostilities in 1937, Japanese pressure against Korean nationalistic activity became so greatly intensified that the *Chŏng'u Tang* (Young Friends Party) was forced to go completely underground. It lost its identity for the remainder of the Japanese occupation period.[13]

The Effectiveness of Ch'ŏndogyo After Son Pyŏng-hi

After the death of Son Pyŏng-hi, the *Sŏngsa,* in May, 1922, Ch'ŏndogyo displayed most of the characteristics typical of resistance movements under tightly controlled colonial regimes. Although the movement continued to be

---

[9]*Ch'ŏndogyo Ch'ang Kŏn Sa,* Pt, IV, pp. 5-7.

[10]Japanese Government General in Korea, Statistical Study No. 42, pp. 939-941.

[11]*Ch'ŏndogyo Chŏngch'i Inyŏm,* p. 39.

[12]Japanese Government General, *op. cit.,* pp. 939-941.

[13]*Ch'ŏndogyo Chŏngch'i Inyŏm,* p. 39.

active, both as a religious cult and as a political-economic-social reform group, leadership was seriously weakened by continuing factionalism resulting from: (a) differing concepts concerning Ch'ŏndogyo policy and administration; (b) divergent attitudes toward relations with the Japanese masters; and (c) petty personal rivalries. Constant and increasing surveillance and restriction by the Japanese authorities prevented the expression or practice of any systematic political philosophy. The same conditions made communications within Ch'ŏndogyo and with other resistance elements extremely hazardous and at best irregular. These conditions would have put even Son Pyŏng-hi, the *Sŏngsa,* to the severest test, but it appears likely that a leader of his genius and his experience with the Japanese could have maintained a more cohesive movement, even in the face of Japanese pressures.

The Technique of the Political Party

As has been indicated earlier in this chapter, the Ch'ŏndogyo Young Friends Party *(Ch'ŏndogyo Chŏng'u Tang)* was organized for the purpose of providing Ch'ŏndogyo members with an ostensibly separate medium for nationalistic activity. Ch'ŏndogyo had from its earliest history been actively interested in political and economic, as well as religious, affairs. Moreover, the political action society had been utilized during the Russo-Japanese War period. However, the society had been narrow in scope and it had been used primarily as a device in effecting collaboration with a foreign power (Japan). It was not until the establishment of the *Ch'ŏndogyo Chŏng'u Tang* after the 1919 uprising, therefore, that Ch'ŏndogyo had available to it a thoroughly organized dual apparatus: an open religious cult which furnished administrative and ideological direction; and a largely covert political party which served as a spearhead of the political, economic, and cultural phases of the movement. This organizational structure was one which offered greater opportunities for undetected nationalistic activities than did a monolithic unit. The actual success achieved through this technique is difficult to assess, because of the understandable lack of detailed information. It is known that the general *Chŏng'u Tang* publication, *Kaebyŏk,* contributed to the cultural development of Korean intellectuals and that the more specialized publications such as *Orini* (Children) also made contributions to the literacy and cultural improvement of the Korean people. It seems safe to assume that the mere existence of *Chŏng'u Tang* groups devoted to the betterment of conditions of women, children, intellectuals, farmers, laborers, and merchants helped to maintain the morale of widely representative Korean groups during the Japanese colonial regime. It is a fact that the *Ch'ŏndogyo Chŏng'u Tang* and the Ch'ŏndogyo sect itself both survived the Japanese period and emerged as active factors in Korean public life in 1945.

CHAPTER VIII
THE HEAVENLY WAY DIVIDED

The Division of Korea

Upon its liberation from Japanese control after the Japanese surrender of August, 1945, Korea found itself occupied by the armed forces of two powerful and mutually antagonistic foreign nations, the United States and the Soviet Union. This dual occupation resulted from a wartime military agreement to use the thirty-eighth parallel of north latitude as a dividing line between American and Soviet zones of responsibility in receiving the surrender of Japanese forces in Korea.

The United States, the United Kingdom, China, and the USSR, in the Cairo and Potsdam Declarations, had pledged that "in due course Korea shall become free and independent." In keeping with this commitment, the American commander, after the surrender of Japanese forces in Korea, initiated negotiations with the Soviet commander looking toward the economic and administrative unification of the country. It soon became apparent to the United States Government, however, that the USSR regarded the thirty-eighth parallel as a rigid partition, and that no relaxation could be effected by local negotiation.[1]

The United States government then took the Korean problem before the Foreign Ministers' conference in Moscow in December, 1945. The resulting Moscow Agreement, to which the United States, the USSR, the United Kingdom, and China were parties, provided for the establishment of a "provisional Korean democratic government." This was to be done on the basis of recommendations worked out by a US-USSR Joint Commission in consultation with "the Korean democratic parties and social organizations," and submitted for the consideration of all the governments adhering to the Moscow Agreement, prior to final decision by the United States and the USSR. The Joint Commission would then consult with the Korean provisional government and the "Korean democratic organizations" in preparing, for the joint consideration of the four governments concerned, recommendations for a four-power trusteeship of Korea for a maximum period of five years.[2]

---

[1]U. S. Dept. of State, *Korea's Independence,* Publication 2933 (Washington: Government Printing Office, 1947), p. 2.

[2]*Ibid.,* pp. 18-19 for full text of Moscow Agreement.

The US-USSR Joint Commission met in Seoul for approximately seven weeks beginning on March 20, 1946, and again, after more than a year's adjournment, for a period of about four months beginning on May 21, 1947. Both series of meetings broke up over Soviet insistence that only those Korean elements which completely endorsed the Moscow Agreement, including its trusteeship provision, were eligible for consultation in the formation of a Korean provisional government. The United States delegation consistently defended the right of all Korean groups to hold and express views opposed to trusteeship, provided they would cooperate with the Joint Commission in its work, including discussion of plans for establishing a trusteeship. Since the dominant, strongly anti-Communist elements in southern Korea had expressed strong opposition to the trusteeship provision of the Moscow Agreement though all recognized groups in the north and Communist-controlled elements in the south had adopted the Soviet position, American acceptance of the Soviet stand would have resulted in the formation of a Communist-dominated coalition government of Korea.[3]

In September, 1947, the United States government, convinced of the futility of further negotiations with the USSR to end the partition of Korea, referred the whole Korean question to the United Nations General Assembly. Despite strenuous opposition by the Soviet Bloc, the General Assembly adopted resolutions providing for general elections in Korea, to be held under the observation of a United Nations commission, to permit the establishment of "a National Government of Korea." When the USSR boycotted all efforts of the commission to implement the General Assembly resolutions in Korea north of the thirty-eighth parallel, the commission was authorized to observe a general election for a Korean National Assembly "in such parts of Korea as are accessible to the Commission." The election was held in southern Korea on May 10, 1948. The elected National Assembly drafted and adopted a constitution providing for a democratic form of government with separation of the three branches, and elected Dr. Syngman Rhee, the strongly anti-Communist veteran of the nationalist movement, first President of the Republic of Korea. The Republic of Korea was formally established on August 15, 1948, and the U.S. Army Military Government ended on the same date. The National Assembly of the Republic of Korea was so constituted as to provide seats for representatives from northern Korea whenever they could be freely elected.

Almost simultaneously with the establishment of the Republic of Korea in the south, a Communist-controlled "Democratic People's Republic of Korea" was established in the north. The Communist leaders in northern Korea, failing in their efforts to block the United Nations-sponsored election in southern Korea, proceeded to hold their own "national" election on August 25, 1948.

---

[3]U. S. Dept. of State, *Korea, 1945 to 1948*, Publication 3305 (Washington: Government Printing Office, 1948), pp. 4-5.

They used a single slate of officially approved candidates, and did not permit the United Nations commission to observe. A supplementary "secret election" was allegedly held in southern Korea to select southern delegates to the "Supreme People's Council."[4]

Thus, by the latter part of 1948, the division of Korea had resulted in the establishment of two ideologically hostile Korean regimes, both claiming to be "national" governments, facing each other across the thirty-eighth parallel. In December, 1948, the United Nations General Assembly approved the elections in southern Korea as representative of the free will of the Korean people and declared the government of the Republic of Korea to be the only lawful government in Korea.[5] In June, 1950, the virtually inevitable clash came when Communist North Korean forces invaded the Republic of Korea.

Internal Social, Economic, and Political Effects of the Division

The highly artificial division of Korea disrupted the normal communications and social patterns of the culturally homogeneous Korean people. It seriously affected the interrelated economy of the country by separating the agriculture and light industry of the south from the heavy industry, mining, and fertilizer production of the north.[6]

Moreover, the division of Korea between the Communist and Free Worlds tended from the first to cause among the Korean people a new polarization of political thoughts and actions. In Korea, where Communism had not previously been strong enough to pose a serious problem, political allegiances had traditionally been based upon loyalty to individual political leaders rather than ideologies. With the division of the country, the new fear of international Communism became the only political issue of sufficient power in the south to attract strong, organized support. In the north, the active Communist leaders, few in number but acting with the strong political and material support of the Soviet authorities, tolerated no anti-Communist groups, and only such non-Communist groups as pledged support for a policy of close cooperation with the Soviet Union.

Any groups which attempted to follow a course between these two political poles became politically ineffective in either the south or north; in the south they were without a political issue of sufficient emotional appeal to attract a significant following, and in the north they were silenced by Communist police-state methods.[7]

---

[4]*Ibid.*, pp. 6-21 for discussion of United Nations handling of the Korean problem; pp. 48-73 for texts of pertinent documents.

[5]U. S. Dept. of State, *The Conflict in Korea,* Publication 4266 (Washington: Government Printing Office, 1951), p. 5.

[6]U. S. Dept. of State, Publication 3305, p. 25; David J. Dallin, *Soviet Russia and the Far East* (New Haven: Yale Univ. Press, 1948), p. 285.

[7]Dallin, *op. cit.,* pp. 286-289; 297-300.

In 1948, all of the small, middle-of-the-road groups in the south, including the southern branch of the *Ch'ŏndogyo Chŏng'u Tang* (Ch'ŏndogyo Young Friends Party), opposed the UN-sponsored election on the ground that such an election would only intensify the division of the country. Although this view was probably sincerely held by at least some of the groups involved, it is also probable that their opposition to the election was motivated in part by a realization that they were not strong enough to win many votes. Shortly before the May election, leaders of these southern groups attended a conference in P'yŏngyang at the invitation of the Communist and pro-Communist leaders in the north, ostensibly to make plans leading toward unification of the country. A communique announcing a decision to continue with unification plans was issued from the conference. However, when, in August, 1948, the northern leaders convoked a second North-South conference and proceeded to establish the "Democratic People's Republic of Korea," twenty-five of the southern groups, including the southern branch of the *Ch'ŏndogyo Chŏng'u Tang,* issued a declaration denouncing the action as contrary to the unification agreement.[8]

The membership, organization, and political status of Ch'ŏndogyo were directly affected by the division of the country. Although Ch'ŏndogyo had originated in extreme southern Korea, there had been a marked shift in its geographical distribution with the result that, by 1945, the large majority of its membership was located in northern Korea. An indication of the proportion can be gained from the fact that *Ch'ŏndogyo Chŏng'u Tang* claimed, in 1946, a total membership of 500,000 and only 80,000 in the American occupation zone.[9] Despite this great preponderance of numerical strength in the north, the national headquarters of Ch'ŏndogyo remained in Seoul, in the southern zone. Under existing conditions, effective central control would have been very difficult, at best. This situation was aggravated by a continuation of the factionalism within Ch'ŏndogyo which had developed in the 1920's after the death of Son Pyŏng-hi, the *Sŏngsa.* In the postwar Korean political atmosphere, the New Faction *(Sin P'a)* was left-of-center in the south and was one of the two non-Communist groups collaborating with the Communist regime in the north. The old Faction *(Ku P'a)* was not permitted to operate in the Communist north, but in the south constituted a small conservative element which, with the support of other, more powerful conservative groups in southern Korea, was able to challenge the New Faction's control of the Seoul central headquarters.[10]

---

[8]Dept. of State Publication 3305, pp. 113-114.

[9]*Ch'ŏndogyo Chŏngch'i Inyŏm,* p. 69; Hq., U. S. Army Military Govt. in Korea, Dept. of Public Information, Bureau of Public Opinion, *Prominent Political Parties in South Korea and Their Tendencies* (Seoul: January, 1948), p. 4.

[10]This material on post-World War II factionalism in Ch'ŏndogyo is based on firsthand information acquired by the writer in Seoul in 1947.

The Political Program

Underlying principles. — It was in the highly unstable and politically charged atmosphere of divided Korea that Ch'ŏndogyo and its political arm, the *Ch'ŏndogyo Chŏng'u Tang* (Ch'ŏndogyo Young Friends Party) had their first opportunity to proclaim a Ch'ŏndogyo political program. The traditional concern of the cult for peaceful social and economic reform set the pattern for its postwar social-economic policies. Its strong nationalist character dictated that its program should appeal to the fundamental Korean desire for a unified, independent Korean government. These basic principles were, in turn, strongly conditioned by the fact that Korea was divided between the Communist and Free Worlds and that this division was directly reflected in Ch'ŏndogyo itself.

The Ch'ŏndogyo program, drawn up in 1947 when the US-USSR Joint Commission was engaged in its fruitless efforts to establish a coalition national government by negotiation, stated the two political missions of Ch'ŏndogyo to be: (1) national emancipation; and (2) social emancipation. The Ch'ŏndogyo policy-makers stated, wishfully, that the first of these missions had been accomplished by the United Nations victory in World War II which had emancipated Korea from Japanese imperialism. The second mission, they said, would not be achieved until the realization of national independence. Ch'ŏndogyo approved of maintaining amicable relations with other countries, since the friendship and help of other nations in making up for Korean deficiencies would be desirable, as long as no limitation was placed thereby upon Korea's sovereignty. It was added, however, that strenuous efforts must be made to remove the impression that Korea is basically dependent upon foreign assistance and influence. The Ch'ŏndogyo policy-makers declared that Koreans had more useful views about democratic principles of politics, economics, and culture than did the leaders of foreign countries. Specifically, they stated: "We do not like American-style free enterprise democracy, since we know the evils of capitalistic institutions. We also do not need the Soviet-style dictatorship of the proletariat." They advocated "Korean-style democracy," characterized by a nondiscriminatory social system. Such a democracy, they said, must have: (1) democratic government and politics; (2) democratic economics; (3) democratic culture; and (4) democratic ethics.[11]

"Democratic government and politics." — The basic principle of this concept, according to the Ch'ŏndogyo platform, was government by, for, and of the people. The platform stated that, although this principle is superficially followed in modern democratic countries such as the United States, the controlling standard is actually the amount of an individual's wealth rather than the quality of the individual. As an illustration of this point, the statement was made that in capitalistic countries the members of the proletariat are ten to one hundred times as numerous as the members of the bourgeois class, and

[11]*Ch'ŏndogyo Chŏngch'i Inyŏm*, pp. 40-43.

yet the members of the proletariat have no rights. Declaring their dislike for "such hypocritical democracy," the Ch'ŏndogyo policy-makers advocated the following bill of rights for "democratic government and politics":

1. All people shall be equal before the law.

2. All people shall have the right to participate in political, economic, cultural, and social life, unless these rights are lost through due process of law.

3. All persons twenty years of age or older shall have the right to vote and to hold office.

4. All persons shall have freedom of speech, press, assembly, organization, religion, study, demonstration, and strike.

5. Except in accordance with the law, all the people shall be free from arrest, imprisonment, questioning, or punishment.

6. All people shall have freedom of residence, and except in accordance with law, there shall be no invasion, search, or closure of a person's home.

7. Except in accordance with law, there shall be no restriction of an individual's freedom of movement.

8. All people shall have the freedom of secrecy of private documents.

9. To the extent permitted by the law, all people shall have the right to possess private property.

10. All people shall be protected in their right to engage in physical and intellectual work.

11. All people shall have the right to receive an elementary education.

12. All people shall have rights of petition.

13. All people shall be entitled to any other civil liberties and rights, so long as the social order or public welfare are not disturbed.

14. People's freedoms and rights shall be limited in so far as necessary in order to: (a) protect the national security; (b) defend the country against emergency; (c) maintain the social order and (d) promote the public welfare.[12]

The Ch'ŏndogyo presentation on "democratic government and politics" included the following three basic observations: First, under "Korean-style democracy," government administrators, legislative representatives, and members of the judiciary must act in the best interests of the people; if they do not, the people must have the right to remove them. Second, this concept of government envisaged equal rights for women, agrarian reform, and the removal of colonial-type economic institutions. Third, since some eighty per cent of the population is composed of workers and farmers, the power of the government must be derived essentially from them.[13]

"Democratic economics." — This economic concept was based on the Ch'ŏndogyo principle of *tong kwi il che* (all life evolves toward a social oneness). In the past, said the Ch'ŏndogyo policy planners, the feudalistic system which prevailed was enjoyed only by the privileged class which controlled the economy. In modern capitalistic society, they added, society is in the hands of the capitalist minority. The proposed "democratic economics" had the purpose of distributing economic privileges equally among the laboring masses. The means of production in agriculture, mining, and industry would be shared among the workers as a result of legal redistribution. Thus the actual producers

---

[12]*Ibid.,* pp. 44-48.   [13]*Ibid.,* pp. 49-51.

would gain a sound position of economic control and the economic privileges of the landlord-capitalist minority would be transferred to the masses. The purpose, said the policy writers, was to establish a unique national economy without class conflict. A government which could enforce this economic system would deserve the name of "democratic government," and the system of politics required to practice it would be genuine "democratic politics."

The right or private ownership of enterprises by the middle class would not, however, be abolished. But in order for such problems to be solved equitably, the democratic economic system and the democratic system of government and politics must be put into effect together as soon as independence had been achieved. At this point, the Ch'ŏndogyo policy-makers attacked the position taken by certain other Korean political elements that the economic order need not be established until after political independence had been achieved. These politicians, declared the Ch'ŏndogyo writers, were either ignorant of the relationship between politics and economics or else blindly determined to extend the capitalistic system. As an illustration of the importance of this interrelationship, the Ch'ŏndogyo planners stated that the solution of the agrarian problem was a fundamental prerequisite of a democratic economic system, and would be the first job of a democratic government.

Two important reasons for the urgency of establishing a democratic economic system, according to the Ch'ŏndogyo policy planners, were: (a) the rapid population increase and (b) the social class structure, characterized by the exploitation of the majority by the landlord minority.

A particularly important requirement of the Korean economy, said the policy writers, was the development of industry along with agricultural improvement. This would have the results of: (a) increasing farm production through application of improved techniques; (b) providing industrial products for use in developing a balanced foreign trade; (c) increasing the productivity of labor; and (d) developing sufficient light industry to satisfy most essential domestic requirements.

This system of democratic economics, the policy-makers emphasized, was not only necessary but also an inevitable historical development for Korea. It was in keeping with the teaching of the Master (Ch'oe Che-u) that the man who keeps his God-given occupation shall be blessed, and that he who does not work should not eat.[14]

"Democratic culture." — The framers of the Ch'ŏndogyo platform declared that, although cultural institutions were normally considered secondary in importance to political and economic ones, in the conditions existing in Korea, democratic culture was a very powerful medium for encouraging the development of democratic political and economic institutions. Ancient Korean culture, they stated, had been brilliant and worthy of the Koreans' pride, but it

---

[14]*Ibid.,* pp. 51-56.

had been restricted to the wealthy and aristocratic classes. Moreover, the modern educational system, though an improvement over the former classical system which had been aimed at preparing a select group for the official examinations, was characterized by the individualism and selfishness of capitalistic economic and political institutions. This educational system, said the Ch'ŏndogyo writers, discriminated against the large proportion of the people who lived in remote villages without schools or, though living in urban centers where there were schools, were unable to pay the fees. The sons and daughters of the rich and aristocratic acquired high school and college certificates even though they were dull, whereas the children of the poor, even though brilliant, were permitted to go uneducated. Regardless of how much effort might be expended under such a system, said the Ch'ŏndogyo policy-makers, human ability could not display itself to the maximum, and human life would be prevented from attaining the highest degree of development.

In accordance with the above analysis of conditions in the cultural field in Korea, Ch'ŏndogyo advocated an educational system founded on the following basic principles: (a) a socialized educational system must be established; (b) educational institutions must be popularized; and (c) a democratized philosophy of education must be insisted upon. Specific measures advanced in the Ch'ŏndogyo program as being necessary to the realization of these principles were: (a) illiteracy must be eradicated; (b) universal compulsory elementary education must be given the most energetic support; and (c) technicians must be developed through special training, so that Korea could build its national economic foundations. In this latter connection, Ch'ŏndogyo also suggested the institution of specialized programs for such purposes as the self-training of laborers and farmers and the elimination of illiteracy among women.

A unique feature of the Ch'ŏndogyo cultural program was its advocacy of *genius education.* A systematic plan for training Korean geniuses was declared to be necessary in order that Korean national prestige and dignity might be bolstered and that Korea might make a contribution to the culture of the world at large. Special laws would be introduced to place upon the whole nation the responsibility of giving geniuses full support until they had achieved success. Selections would be made throughout the nation, with a view to discovering all those who were truly geniuses. The Ch'ŏndogyo writers felt certain that in such a way scholars, technicians, and inventors of world-wide renown could be produced from within the Korean nation.

The Ch'ŏndogyo platform-writers stated that in the past, the fields of music and literature in Korea had been only for the minority (officials and the wealthy). Dancing and singing, they stated, had been performed only by the *kisaeng* (professional female entertainers), and the *kisaeng* had been preempted by the official-wealthy minority. Likewise in Korean literature, said the writers, the characteristic themes had been such as that of the well-known novel *Ch'unhyang Chŏn* (Story of Ch'unhyang): that Korean girls must maintain their chastity for the benefit of members of the official-wealthy minority and their sons. Ch'ŏndogyo declared that "such artificial standards for music and literature must be destroyed and that a realistic foundation for Korean music and literature must be established on the basis of the actual life of the people: people's sighs, people's laughter, people's hunger, and people's poverty."[15]

"Democratic ethics." — Democratic ethics, according to the Ch'ŏndogyo policy-framers, was just as necessary as democratic government, democratic economics, or democratic culture. The classical (Confucian) ethics, they stated, had been based upon class distinctions and therefore had established unequal ethical standards. Modern democratic ethics, they reasoned, should be based entirely on individuality and on equal ethical standards. Democratic ethics (the traditional Ch'ŏndogyo ethics discussed in Chapter II, above) had as its basis the principle of *sa in yŏ ch'ŏn* (treat people as though they were God). *Sa in yŏ ch'ŏn* encompassed the virtues of sincerity, respect, and faith. Sincerity, in turn, embraced truth, diligence, and energy. Respect involved respect for heaven, respect for man, and respect for things. Faith, according to the principle of *sa in yŏ ch'ŏn,* was thought of as embracing actions of complete honesty and personal loyalty in human relations without discrimination. This type of relationship was contrasted, by the Ch'ŏndogyo writers, with the traditional Korean relationships. For example, they said, members of the official-scholar class had been honest among themselves and landlords had been honest to other landlords, but the official or scholar had not practiced honesty in his dealings with the common people and the landlord had not been honest with the tenant.[16]

Effectiveness of the Program

The "Korean-style democracy" advocated by Ch'ŏndogyo in its post-World War II political platform never was put into practice as a government program and must therefore be criticized largely in the abstract. In retrospect, the idea of rejecting both the American and Soviet patterns in proposing a form of government for Korea under conditions then existing appears naïve. Yet, no other approach would have been politically feasible for Ch'ŏndogyo, because: (a) the cult had a long nationalist-reformist tradition and therefore, to be in character, would have to advocate a program of political, economic, and social changes within a Korean framework; (b) Ch'ŏndogyo could not publicly adopt either the American or the Soviet system and continue to operate freely in both parts of Korea; and (c) at the time the platform was drawn up, the US-USSR Joint Commission was attempting to establish a coalition national government, and because of the mutual antipathy of the American and Soviet philosophies of government, some "Korean" compromise formula was a logical possibility.

---

[15]*Ibid.,* pp. 57-60.   [16]*Ibid.,* pp. 62-65.

The argumentation given to demonstrate that American democracy is "hypo-critical" could well have come from a Communist textbook. But the fourteen-point bill of rights contains many points in common with the American Bill of Rights. It is noted in Point Nine, however, that people are to enjoy the right of possessing private property "to the extent permitted by the law." Although this qualification may have been inserted for the sake of consistency with the Ch'ŏndogyo economic policy of nationalization, it is the type of loophole which enabled the Communists in northern Korea to subvert the Ch'ŏndogyo philosophy and program to Communist purposes. Point Fourteen, also, in the hands of Communists or other unprincipled rulers, could be so abused as to negate all of the rights enumerated in the other thirteen points. That the Com-munists did, in fact, subvert Ch'ŏndogyo to their own purposes in northern Korea is clearly demonstrated in a story by two Soviet writers who visited the area in 1946. This account referred to Ch'ŏndogyo as "one of the active forces in liberated Korea." Ch'oe Che-u, the founder of Ch'ŏndogyo, is said to have advocated a society in which "there will never be classes or estates." Ch'oe Si-hyŏng, the *Sinsa,* is characterized as the "Korean Pugachev" after a famous Russian peasant revolt leader.[17]

The Ch'ŏndogyo proposals for "democratic economics" are confused and are phrased in language which indicates considerable Marxist influence. It is true that this economic program is addressed to the solution of fundamental economic problems of long standing, and, in some of its principal features, appears hardly more leftist than that drawn up in 1946 by Dr. Syngman Rhee and approved by most other conservative leaders. Among other things, this program of the conservatives provided for: (a) nationalization of all heavy in-dustry, mines, forests, public utilities, banks, railways, water power, fisheries, communication and transportation systems, and public health facilities; (b) inauguration of state supervision of all commercial and industrial enterprises; (c) enactment of liberal wage and hour legislation; (d) redistribution of all con-fiscated [Japanese] agricultural lands to small farmers; (e) control of charges made by private loan agencies and abolishment of private pawnshops.[18] How-ever, in the techniques advocated for implementing its economic objectives, the Ch'ŏndogyo economic program, if not Marxist-motivated, is so framed as to invite Communist exploitation. This is particularly true of the proposal to transfer economic control from the "landlord-capitalist minority" to the "masses" by means of "legal redistribution."

The Ch'ŏndogyo statement on "democratic culture" is subject to the same type of evaluation as the other phases of the program. The presentation of past evils in education and other cultural fields is essentially sound, but the entire

[17]A. Gitovich and B. Bursov (Trans. George Leonof), *North of the 38th Parallel* (Shanghai: Epoch Publishing Co., 1948), pp. 117-121.

[18]Henry Chung, *The Russians Came to Korea* (Washington: Korean Pacific Press, 1947), pp. 207-210.

cultural plan is so nebulously worded that it could be adopted by the Communists without significant change.

The "democratic ethics" of Ch'ŏndogyo contains the idealism which has always distinguished it from the old Oriental systems of religion and ethics and, more recently, from Communism. However, the ethical system alone, without the rituals and religious zeal which formerly gave it unique strength, was not sufficiently dynamic to enable Ch'ŏndogyo to play a strong, positive role in Korea in the period 1945-1950.

Evaluation of Ch'ŏndogyo Actions After World War II

The removal of the pressures associated with the long Japanese colonial control of Korea and the emergence of new, conflicting pressures in the postwar period appear to have left Ch'ŏndogyo without the ability or will to devise any·new techniques or to employ any of its previously used techniques effectively. In order for a technique to be effective under conditions prevailing in postwar Korea, it would have had to be a dramatic one, such as: (a) the technique of armed rebellion, used in the Tonghak period; or (b) the technique of nonviolent rebellion, used in 1919 in the period of Japanese control. Armed rebellion, even if feasible in the postwar period, probably would have been considered by Ch'ŏndogyo leaders to be inconsistent with the objective of national unity. Nonviolent rebellion against certain blatantly anti-Korean measures of the Communist regime in northern Korea would have been less inconsistent and, at the same time, might have been feasible and sufficiently effective to encourage other non-Communist elements in the north to follow nationalistic rather than Communist-approved policies.

The course actually followed by Ch'ŏndogyo in northern Korea was one of collaboration with the Communists. The *Ch'ŏndogyo Chŏng'u Tang* (Ch'ŏndogyo Young Friends Party) was one of the two non-Communist political parties in northern Korea which were recognized and included in the Communist-controlled political front. The reasoning behind this collaboration can only be surmised. It may be that the Ch'ŏndogyo leaders in the north were deluded, at least initially, into believing that Communists would adopt a Ch'ŏndogyo-type popular reform program. It may be that the Ch'ŏndogyo leaders, perhaps in the hope that Communist control would be short-lived, decided it was more important to save the organization than to stand firmly on nationalistic Korean principles. It could also be that certain of the Ch'ŏndogyo leaders had become Communist-oriented during the period of resistance to the Japanese and deliberately led Ch'ŏndogyo into a course of collaboration designed to advance Communist interests.

In southern Korea, as has been seen, Ch'ŏndogyo attempted to steer a middle course politically. It was rendered ineffectual, however, by its own internal factionalism and by the overwhelming pressures exerted by the presence of the large Ch'ŏndogyo element in the Communist north, on the one hand, and by the powerful force of southern Korean anti-Communist nationalism on the other.

CHAPTER IX
THE FINAL RECKONING

Strengths and Weaknesses of Principles and Program

The idealistic doctrine of Ch'oe Che-u, which formed the foundation of all the ideological principles of Ch'ŏndogyo, contained many of the dynamic qualities essential to a successful nationalist movement dedicated to sweeping domestic reforms or to the restoration of political independence. The basic principle *in nae ch'ŏn* (Man and God are one) and the other principles derived from it carried tremendous meaning for the vast majority of Koreans who, particularly in the second half of the nineteenth century, lived under political-economic-social oppression and inequality which were characteristic of Oriental despotism at its worst. The doctrine itself, together with the mysticism and ritual associated with it, gave a needed hope and unity of purpose to a large element of Koreans who had had no dynamic religion and whose condition of life had appeared hopeless.

The original inspirational doctrine of Ch'oe Che-u was translated into more practical terms by his successors, Ch'oe Si-hyŏng and Son Pyŏng-hi. If man truly had within him divine potentialities, then he, in concert with his fellows, had the ability eventually to change his oppressive environment through an evolutionary process of popular reform. The principles of *sa in yŏ ch'ŏn* (treat people as though they were God) and *tong kwi il ch'e* (all life evolves toward a social oneness) formed the basis for a completely new set of standards for Korean ethical, social, economic, and political life, embodying such reforms as: (a) equalization of standards of conduct and social privileges; (b) amelioration of the economic conditions of tenant farmers and small shopkeepers; and (c) institution of more benevolence in the administration and dispensation of justice by the government.

During the Tonghak period, when the movement was directed toward reform of the existing Korean Government, the doctrine, ritual, and program of Ch'ŏndogyo provided a basis for concrete reformist activity which was able to achieve some local successes despite almost overwhelming odds. During the period of Japanese control, there was no real prospect of achieving the desired reforms, and the restoration of Korean independence became the immediate objective of Ch'ŏndogyo. In these circumstances, under the skillful leadership of Son Pyŏng-hi, the *Sŏngsa,* the doctrine and ritual served as an effective vehicle for the development of *esprit de corps* in the Ch'ŏndogyo movement.

A principal weakness of the Ch'ŏndogyo doctrine and program was that they appealed to the underprivileged, oppressed majority, almost to the exclusion of members of the Korean upper class who were also interested in reform. This fact, and the development of antiforeignism in the Ch'ŏndogyo movement just prior to the Tonghak Rebellion of 1894, may have been responsible for the lack of coordination between the Tonghak reformers and the small but able Western-oriented reform group which was active in Seoul during the same period. Another weakness was that the Ch'ŏndogyo doctrine and program derived their main force from a situation of opposition to a despotic ruling group or a foreign colonial regime. This weakness of Ch'ŏndogyo's ideological base became apparent following the end of Japanese occupation in 1945 and was at least partly responsible for the ineffectual performance of the cult in the 1945-1950 period. Perhaps the most important weakness of the ideological principles of Ch'ŏndogyo was that the language and concepts used in their formulation were so all-inclusive and imprecise as to invite the subversion of the movement by ruthless elements. In the 1890's, the rebel leader Chŏn Pong-jin was able to take advantage of the antigovernment position of the Tonghak movement to gain the support of a substantial portion of its members in a resort to armed rebellion contrary to the basic Tonghak principles. In the period during and immediately following the Russo-Japanese War, the pro-Japanese leader Yi Yong-gu succeeded for a time in subverting the Tonghak reform program to serve the interests of the Japanese "reformers." In divided Korea following World War II, the nebulous Ch'ŏndogyo program facilitated the subversion of the movement in northern Korea by the Communists.

Evaluation of Ch'ŏndogyo Techniques

During the period 1860-1950, the life span of Ch'ŏndogyo as an active element in Korean political life, six identifiable techniques were employed, not including the negative and disastrous technique of accommodation to Communism in northern Korea after 1945. These six techniques were: (1) *passive reform,* employed during most of the Tonghak period and maintained as an objective during the period of Japanese control; (2) *nonviolent rebellion,* practiced in the independence demonstration of 1919, during the period of Japanese control; (3) *armed rebellion,* employed in the Tonghak period; (4) *the technique of the political party,* utilized during the period of Japanese control after the 1919 uprising; (5) *petitioning the government,* used during the Tonghak period, prior to the Tonghak Rebellion and prior to the outbreak of the Russo-Japanese War; and (6) *collaboration with a foreign power* (Japan), advocated and partly implemented in the latter part of the Tonghak period.

The *passive reform* technique of Ch'ŏndogyo, though only partly successful in accomplishing the desired reforms, achieved notable success in building up an effective organization at local, provincial, and national levels. During the

Tonghak period, when the movement was officially proscribed, major emphasis was placed on strong local groups, responsive to general direction from higher headquarters. In the period of Japanese control, when Son Pyŏng-hi, the *Sŏngsa,* was rebuilding the Ch'ŏndogyo organization and saw the need for centralized control, he successfully utilized the same organizational structure, but changed the emphasis from the local group to national and regional headquarters.

The technique of *nonviolent rebellion* achieved its immediate objective of attracting world attention to the issue of Korean independence, and it also was a major factor in the development of a strong Korean national spirit. This technique was not sufficient to achieve Korean independence, because of the strong desire of the principal world powers, after World War I, to maintain friendly relations with Japan and avoid further warfare.

Armed rebellion, which was not in accordance with Ch'ŏndogyo principles, achieved remarkable success in the early stages of the Tonghak Rebellion, but ultimately proved disastrous. Among the principal reasons for this failure were: (a) serious factionalism within the Tonghak movement over the use of armed force; (b) failure of the advancing Tonghak forces to live up to their high principles of conduct; and (c) lack of understanding, among the Tonghak leaders, of the realities of international politics.

The effectiveness of *the technique of the political party* cannot be fully evaluated, because of insufficient information on Ch'ŏndogyo activities after 1919. The maintenance of a dual, religio-political organization was potentially a valuable technique during the Japanese control period, when religious groups retained a degree of freedom but when all nationalist activities had to be conducted covertly. However, available information tends to indicate that the *Ch'ŏndogyo Chŏng'u Tang* (Ch'ŏndogyo Young Friends Party) was under effective surveillance by the Japanese authorities, and therefore was able to carry out little political activity. Its principal known accomplishment was the publication of general and specialized publications which made a contribution to Korean cultural development during the period of Japanese control.

Petitioning the government was a significant technique during the Tonghak period because its use identified the Tonghak organization as a group of loyal Korean subjects, seeking redress for grievances in the traditional manner. However, the petitioning accomplished nothing but to convince the more extremist Tonghak elements that more forceful measures were necessary.

Collaboration with a foreign power (Japan) was a logical technique for Ch'ŏndogyo to follow between the defeat of the Tonghak Rebellion (1894) and the establishment of the Japanese protectorate over Korea (1905). If Son Pyŏng-hi, the *Sŏngsa,* had maintained firm control of his organization during this period, the policy of collaboration might have been directed in such a way as to benefit Ch'ŏndogyo and Korea. As a matter of fact, however, this collaboration, effected through the *Ilchin Hoe* (Advancement Society), benefited only the Japanese and all but wrecked the *Sŏngsa*'s Ch'ŏndogyo organization.

Evaluation of Ch'ŏndogyo Leadership

The principal strength of the Ch'ŏndogyo movement was the leadership provided by its three outstanding figures. Ch'oe Che-u, the *Taesinsa*, gave the movement its doctrinal foundation and reformist spirit; Ch'oe Si-hyŏng, the *Sinsa*, gave the Master's ideals practical application and established the organization which was the foundation of the relatively successful technique of passive reform; and Son Pyŏng-hi, the *Sŏngsa*, carried on and adapted the organizational and doctrinal work of his predecessor in such a way as to make Ch'ŏndogyo the leading force in the nonviolent rebellion against Japanese control.

The efficient organizational structure developed by Ch'ŏndogyo in the Tonghak period and perfected during the period of Japanese control contributed materially to the success of the nonviolent rebellion of 1919, by providing speedy and secure communications between the national level and the local unit. The financial resources of the Ch'ŏndogyo organization, accumulated through the *Sŏngmi* (Sincerity Rice) System, supported the entire uprising.

The political genius and administrative ability of Son Pyŏng-hi, the *Sŏngsa*, made him one of the great leaders of modern Korean nationalism. He was the principal leader of the uprising of March 1, 1919, which gave birth to the Korean independence movement.

Ch'ŏndogyo also provided an important object lesson through its failures. The great importance to a nationalist movement of strong, dedicated leadership and clear, unequivocal political principles and platforms was clearly demonstrated by the disastrous results experienced by Ch'ŏndogyo when these factors were absent.

ALPHABETICAL LISTING OF KOREAN, CHINESE, AND JAPANESE WORDS AND PHRASES, WITH IDEOGRAPHS

The Sacred Formula
Infinite Energy being now within me, I yearn that it may
pour into all living beings and created things.
Since this Infinite Energy abides in me, I am identified
with God, and of one nature with all existence.
Should I ever forget these things, all existing things will
know of it.

An Ch'ang-ho (安昌浩) Korean nationalist leader; founder of
the *Sinmin Hoe*

Ch'amwisŏl (讖緯說) Theory of Interpretation of Omens

Ch'anggi (唱妓) Professional entertainer

Chi (智) Knowledge

Chi Il (地 日) Earth Day

Chibang Bu (地方部) District Branch

Ch'il Ch'ŏn (七 賤) Seven Lowest Official Occupations

Chinbo Hoe (進步會) Progressive Society

Ch'ing (清) Manchu Dynasty in China, 1644-1912

Chipkang (執綱) Judge

Chiri (智異) Mountain in southwestern Korea

Chisang ch'ŏn'guk (地上天國) Heaven on Earth

Chisang ch'ŏn'guk kŏnsŏl (地上天國建設) Establishment of
Heaven on Earth

Cho Pyŏng-sik (趙秉式) Governor of Ch'ungch'ŏng Province

Ch'oe Che-u (崔濟愚) Founder of Ch'ŏndogyo

Ch'oe Nam-sŏn (崔南善) Prominent Korean historian and a planner of the 1919 independence uprising

Ch'oe Si-hyŏng (崔時亨) The second great leader of Ch'ŏndogyo

§ *103* §

Ch'oe Rin (崔 麟) A Ch'ŏndogyo leader and a principal planner of the 1919 uprising

Chogun (漕 軍) Oarsman

Chojik Bu (組織部) Organization Department

Chŏlla (全羅) Southwestern province of Korea

Ch'ŏn Il (天日) Heaven Day

Chŏn Pong-jun (全琫準) Leader of the Tonghak Rebellion

Chŏmbok (占卜) Fortune teller

Ch'ŏndogyo (天道教) Religion of the Heavenly Way

Ch'ŏndogyo Ch'ŏngnyŏn Hoe (天道教青年會) Ch'ŏndogyo Youth Society

Ch'ŏndogyo Ch'ŏngnyŏn Kyori Kangyŏn Bu (天道教青年教理講演部) Ch'ŏndogyo Youth Department for study of the Doctrine

Ch'ŏndogyo Chŏng'u Tang (天道教青友黨) Ch'ŏndogyo Young Friends Party

Chŏng (情) Love

Chŏng Ki-hyŏn (鄭基鉉) Associate of Yi P'il in the 1871 revolt

Chŏng Wŏn (政院) Royal Board of Registry

Ch'ongdok (總督) Governor General

Chonggyo ŭi Chŏngŭi (宗教의定義)Definition of Religion

Chongjŏng (宗正) Censor

Ch'ŏngju (清州) Important center in Ch'ungch'ŏng province

Ch'ongmu Bu (總務部) General affairs Department

Chongnisa Ch'ong Hoe (總理事總會) General Assembly

Ch'ŏngnyŏn Bu (青年部) Youth Department

Ch'ŏngnyŏn Hoe (青年會) Youth Society

Ch'ŏngsan (青山) Town in Ch'ungch'ŏng Province

Ch'ŏngsu (淨水) Pure water

Ch'ŏnju (全州) Capital of Chŏlla Province

Ch'ŏnju (天主) Lord of Heaven

Chosŏn Nodong Sa (朝鮮勞働社) Korean Labor Institute

Chosŏn Nongmin Sa (朝鮮農民社) Korean Farmers' Institute

Chŏp (接) Local Ch'ŏndogyo unit

Chŏpchu (接主) Leader of a local Ch'ŏndogyo unit

Ch'uije (取才) "Selection of the skilled," a government examination for professional specialists

Chugan P'odŭksa (主幹布德師) Principal Spiritual Leader

Chumun (呪文) Ritual

Ch'unam (春菴) Honorific name of Pak In-ho

Chung'ang Chip'haeng Central Executive Committee
  Wiwŏnhoe (中央執行委員會)

Ch'ungch'ŏng (忠清) Province in south central Korea

Chung'in (中人) "Middle people," the designation of a special class

Chungjong (中宗) Yi Dynasty king, 1505-1544

Chungnip Hoe (中立會) Neutrality Society

Chunhyang Chŏn (春香傳) *Story of Chunhyang*

Genyōsha (玄洋社) The Japanese "Dark Ocean Society"

Haewŏl (海月) Honorific for Ch'oe Si-hyŏng

Haksaeng Bu (學生部) Student Department

Haksaeng Hoe (學生會) Students' Society

Haksul Yŏn'gu Bu (學說研究部) Academic Research Department

Ham T'ae-yŏng (咸台永) Prominent Christian leader in the 1919 independence uprising

Hamgyŏng (咸鏡) Province in northeastern Korea

Han (漢) Chinese Dynasty, 202 B.C.-9 A.D.

Han Yong-un (韓龍雲) Buddhist leader in the 1919 Independence uprising

Hanŭl (하늘) Heaven

Hideyoshi (秀吉) Ruler of Japan, 1587-1598

Hong Kye-hun (洪啓薰) Korean Government Military Commander

Hullyŏn Bu (訓練部) Training Department

Hwanghae (黄 海) West coast province of Korea

Hwangje (皇 帝) King

Hyŏn Sang-yun (玄 相 允) One of the planners of the 1919 uprising

Ilchin Hoe (一 進 會) Advancement Society

Ilsu (日 守) Watchman

In Il (人 日) Man Day

In nae ch'ŏn (人 乃 天) Man and God are one

Inch'ŏn (仁 川) Yellow Sea port, near Seoul

Isin Hwan sŏng (以 身 換 性) Sacrifice of the physical for the spiritual

Ito Hirobumi (伊 藤 博 文) Prince; Japanese Resident-General in Korea, 1906-1909

Kaebyŏk (開 闢) *Creation*: official journal of Ch'ŏndogyo

Kaehwa (開 化) "Enlightment": name of a Korean reform party in the late 1800's

Kaejŏp (開 接) Worship

Kakse chin'gyŏng (覺 世 眞 經) Code of Enlightment

Kamsan (甘 山) Town in Kyŏngsang Province

Kangwŏn (江 原) Korean east coast province

Kayasa (伽 倻 寺) Famous Korean Buddhist temple

Kido (祈 禱) Prayer

Kil Sŏn-ju (吉 善 宙) Prominent Presbyterian minister; a leader of the 1919 independence uprising

Kim Kae-nam (金 開 南) A principal lieutenant of Chŏn Pong-jun in the Tonghak Rebellion

Kim Ok-kyun (金 玉 均) Korean reformist leader, murdered by the pro-Chinese Korean Government faction

Kim Yŏn-guk (金 演 局) A leading signer of the Tonghak petition to the King

Kimm Kiusic (金 奎 植) Prominent Korean nationalist leader;
[Kim Kyu-sik] delegate of the Korean provisional Government who unsuccessfully sought a hearing at the Paris Peace Conference

Kisaeng (妓 生) Professional female entertainer

Kobu (古 阜) County in Chŏlla Province; starting point of the
Tonghak Rebellion

Kongju (公 州) Capital of Ch'ungch'ŏng Province

Kongno (公 奴) Official slave

Ku P'a (舊 派) Old Faction

Kun (郡) County

Kung (弓) A key character of the Sacred Formula of Ch'ŏndogyo

Kunsu (郡 守) County Chief Magistrate

Kwagŏ (科 擧) State examinations for the civil and military services

Kwangdae (廣 大) Artists and acrobats

Kwangje Ch'angsaeng (廣 濟 蒼 生) General Equality of the
People

Kwangmu (光 武) Emperor; next to last ruler of the Yi Dynasty

Kwŏn Tong-jin (權 東 鎭) A prominent leader in the independence
uprising of 1919

Kyojang (校 長) Chief Instructor

Kyojŏng Ilch'i (敎 宗 一 致) Consistency of Religion and Politics

Kyŏnggi (京 畿) The Capital Province of Korea

Kyŏngju (慶 州) Ancient capital of the Kingdom of Silla in southeastern Korea; the principal center of the region
in which the Ch'ŏndogyo movement began

Kyŏngsang (慶 尙) Province in southeastern Korea

Kyori Kangsŭpso (敎 理 講 習 所) Religious Training Institute

Kyosu (敎 授) Teacher

Kyumo Ilch'i (規 模 一 致) Uniformity of Discipline

Li Hung-chang (李 鴻 章) Chinese Viceroy in the latter part of the
19th century

Min (閔) The family of the Korean Queen in the latter part of the
Yi Dynasty

Ming (明) Chinese Dynasty, 1368-1644

Mugyŏk (誣 告) Sorcerers and sorceresses

Mujang (茂 長) County in Chŏlla Province

Mun'gyŏng (聞 慶) Town in southeastern Korea; birth place of
Yi P'il, leader of the 1871 revolt

Nae Sudomun (內 修道文) Inner Rules of Conduct

Najang (羅 將) Guard

Nam Ho-won (南 弘 源) A skilled Ch'ŏndogyo calligrapher

Namjŏp (南 接) Southern Jurisdiction

Nodong Bu (勞 働 部) Labor Department

Nongmin (農 民) *Farmer*, a Ch'ŏndogyo publication

Nongmin Bu (農 民 部) Farmer's Department

Nongmin kongsaeng chohap (農民共生組合) Farmers' cooperative

Nongmin Sesang (農民世上) *Farmers' World*, a Ch'ŏndogyo
publication

Noron (老 論) Ruling *yangban* faction in Korea during the latter
part of the Yi Dynasty

O Chi-yŏng (吳 致 吳) Tonghak leader who mediated between the
orthodox and rebel factions

O Se-chang (吳 世 昌) A prominent leader in the 1919 uprising

O Yŏng Ch'ang (吳 榮 昌) Leader of the Ku P'a or "Old Faction"
of Ch'ŏndogyo, formed in 1925

O Yun-jung (魚 允 仲) Respected Korean cabinet minister

Orini (어린이) *Children*, a Ch'ŏndogyo publication

Osim Tang (吾心黨) "Our Heart Party", an underground group

Paek Yong-sŏng (白龍成) Buddhist leader in 1919 Independence
demonstration

Paekchŏng (白 丁) Butchers

Pak Hi-do (朴希道) A prominent Christian leader in the 1919
independence uprising

Pak In-ho (朴寅浩) Son Pyong-hi's successor as leader of
Ch'ŏndogyo

Pak Kwang-ho (朴光浩) Chief signer of the Tonghak petition to
the King

P'al Ban (八 賤) Eight Socially Degraded Groups

Pannyo (搬 僚) Official messengers

P'o (布) Local congregation

P'odŏk ch'ŏnha (布 德 天 下) Propagation of the faith throughout the world

P'odŏksa (布 德 師) Spiritual leader

Poguk Anmin (保 國 安 民) Welfare of the country and safety for the people

Poho (保 護) Protection

Po i and Shu ch'i (伯 夷 와 叔 齊) Brothers renowned in Chinese legendary history for their integrity and faithfulness

Ponggun (烽 軍) Torch guard

Pŏp Hoe (法 會) Ecclesiastical Assembly

Pŏp Taedoju (法 大 道 主) Supreme leader of the Way

Posŏng (善 成) Name of Ch'ŏndogyo educational institutions

Pottari (보 따 리) "Bundle," a nickname for Ch'oe Si-hyŏng

Poŭn (報 恩) Town in Ch'ungch'ŏng Province, used as a Tonghak convention site

Puan (扶 安) County in Chŏlla Province

Pukchŏp (北 接) "Northern Jurisdiction," the areas which remained loyal to the orthodox Tonghak leadership during the Tonghak Rebellion

Pulpul Tang (不 不 黨) "Double Negative" Party, an underground arm of Ch'ŏndogyo

P'yŏngan (平 安) Northwestern Korean Province

Pyŏngbu (兵 符) Reed symbolizing royal authority

P'yŏngyang (平 壤) Principal city of northwestern Korea

Rhee, Syngman [Yi Sung-man] (李 承 晩) First President of the Korean Provisional Government and first President of the Republic of Korea

Sa in yŏ ch'ŏn (事 人 如 天) Treat People as Though They were God

Samnye (參 禮) Town in southwestern Korea

Sangje (上 帝) "Superior Ruler," a designation for God

Sangju (尙 州) Town in southeastern Korea

Sangmin Bu (商 民 部) Merchants' Department

Sano (私 奴) Private slave

Seoul [Sŏul] (서 울) Capital of Korea since the beginning of the
　　　　　　Yi Dynasty (1392)

Sich'ŏn'gyo (侍天教) "Serve Heaven Cult," a splinter group
　　　　　　formed by dissident, Japanese-aligned
　　　　　　elements of Ch'ŏndogyo

Siil (侍 日) Rest Day

Silla (新 羅) Ancient Kingdom in southeastern Korea

Sin Hong-sik (申 弘 植) Prominent Methodist minister who played
　　　　　　a leading role in the 1919 uprising

Sin P'a (新 派) New Faction

Sin Yŏsŏng (新女性) *New Womanhood,* a Chŏndogyo
　　　　　　publication

Sinang Tongil (信仰統 一) Unity of Faith

Sinmin Hoe (新 民 會) New People's Society

Sinsa (神 師) "Divine Teacher," official title of Ch'oe Sihyŏng,
　　　　　　the second great leader in Ch'ŏndogyo

Sŏ Chang-ok (徐 昌 玉) Tonghak rebel leader in Ch'ungch'ŏng
　　　　　　Province

Sŏ In-ju (徐 仁 周) A Tonghak advocate of forceful action

Sŏ Pyŏng-hak (徐 丙 鶴) An associate of Sŏ In-ju in advocating
　　　　　　forceful action by Tonghak

Sŏhak (西 學) "Western Learning," a designation for Christianity

Son Ch'ŏn-min (孫 天 民) A leading signer of Tonghak petition to
　　　　　　the King

Son Hwa-jung (孫 華 仲) A principal lieutenant of Ch'ŏn Pong-jun,
　　　　　　the Tonghak rebel leader

Son Pyŏng-hi (孫 秉 熙) The third great leader of Ch'ŏndogyo

Son Pyŏng-hŭm (孫 秉 欽) Brother and associate of Son Pyŏng-hi

Song Chin-u (宋 鎭 禹) One of the planners of the 1919 uprising

Song Pyŏng-jun (宋 秉 畯) A leader of the Japanese aligned faction
　　　　　　of Ch'ŏndogyo which was expelled and
　　　　　　formed the splinter group, Sich'ŏn'gyo

Sŏngmi (聖 米) "Sincerity Rice," contributed by Ch'ŏndogyo members for the support of the cult

Sŏngsa (聖 師) "Holy Teacher," official title of Son Pyŏng-hi, the third great leader of Ch'ŏndogyo

Sŏngsin Ssangjŏn (性身雙全) Unity of Mind and Matter

Sŏngnyŏng Ch'ulsesŏl (聖靈出世說) Doctrine of the Transmigration of the Spirit

Sŏnjŏn Bu (宣傳部) Propaganda Department

Sŏnsaeng (先生) Teacher

Sugun (水軍) Sailor

Sui (隋) Chinese Dynasty, 581-618 A.D.

Sŭngi (僧尼) Buddhist priests and nuns

Suun (水雲) Honorific for Ch'oe Che-u

Tae Kyokuje (大教區制) Religious District System

Taebaek (太白) Korean east coast mountain range

Taejongsa (大宗司) Central Control Office

Taedong Hoe (大同會) Great East Society

Taegu (大邱) City in southeastern Korea, capital of the modern North Kyŏngsang Province

T'aein (泰仁) County in Chŏlla Province

Taejong (大宗) Counselor

Taesinsa (大神師) "Great Divine Teacher," the official title of Ch'oe Che-u, the founder of Ch'ŏndogyo

Taewŏn'gun (大院君) Title of the Korean Regent

Taip'ing (太平) Anti-imperial movement in China, 1850-64

Tamura (田村) A Japanese General in Korea prior to the Russo-Japanese War

T'ang (唐) Chinese Dynasty, 618-907 A.D.

Tang Ponbu (黨本部) Party Headquarters

Tenyūkyo (天理教) "Heaven-guided Group," a Japanese nationalist society

Terauchi (寺內) General; first Japanese Governor-General of Korea

To (道) The Way

Tojip (道 執) Chief Administrator

Tojŏpju (道 接主) District Leader of Ch'ŏndogyo

Toju (道 主) Provincial leader of Ch'ŏndogyo

Toju (道 主) Leader of the Way; Master

Toju Kinyŏmil (道主 記念日) Anniversary of the Master

Tong kwi il che (同 歸 一 體) All life Evolves Toward a Social Oneness

Tongdŏk (同 德) Name of a Ch'ŏndogyo girls' high school

Tonghak (東 學) "Eastern Learning," the designation of Ch'ŏndogyo prior to December, 1905

Tongil Kisŏng Hoe (統 一 期成會) Society to Carry Out Unification

Tongnip Hyŏphoe (獨立 協會) Independence Club

Toryŏng (道 領) Leader of the Way

Tosasil (道事室) Office of the Affairs of the Way

Uchida Ryohei (內 田 良 平) Japanese ultra-nationalist leader

Ui (意) Will

Uiam (芉 菴) Honorific name of Son Pyŏng-hi

Uipyŏngdae (義兵隊) Righteous Army

Ul (乙) A key character in the sacred formula of Ch'ŏndogyo

Yang tzŭ and Mo tzŭ (揚子 와 墨子) Unorthodox Chinese Philosophers

BIBLIOGRAPHY

Aeguk Tongji Wŏnhohoe (The Relief Society for Patriotic Compatriots). *Hanguk Tong-nip Undongsa* (History of Korean Independence Movement). Seoul: 1956.

Akagi, Roy H. *Japan's Foreign Relations*. Tokyo: Hukuseido, 1937.

Aoyagi, Nammei. *Chōsen Dokuritsu Shōyō Shiron* (An Historical Account of Korea's Independence Disturbance). Seoul: Korea, Statistical Assn., 1921.

Aoyagi, Nammei. *Chōsen Shiwa to Shiseki* (Korean Historical Tales and Places). 5th ed. Seoul: Korean Research Society,. 1928.

Bemis, Samuel F. *A Diplomatic History of the United States*. Revised Edition. New York: Holt, 1942.

Blakeslee, George H. (ed.). *China and the Far East*. New York: Crowell, 1910.

Bonsal, Stephen. *Suitors and Suppliants*. New York: Prentice Hall, 1946.

British and Foreign State Papers, Vol. LXVII.

Cameron, M. E., T. H. D. Mahoney, and G. E. McReynolds, *China, Japan and the Powers*. 2 Vols. New York: Ronald Press, 1952.

Carnegie Endowment for International Peace. Pamphlet No. 43. *Korea: Treaties and Agreements*. Washington: 1921.

Cho, Chong-o. *Chosŏn Ch'aegŭn Samdae Undongsa* (A History of The Three Largest Movements in Korea in Recent Times). Seoul: Ungbyŏn Kurakpu Ch'ulp'anbu, 1946.

Ch'ŏn, Kwan-u. "Kabo Kyŏngjang Kwa Kundaehwa" (The Reforms and Moderniza-tion of 1894). Sasanggye, December, 1954, pp. 8-39.

Ch'ŏndogyo Ch'ang Kŏn Sa. (History of the Origin and Establishment of Ch'ŏndogyo). Seoul: Taedong Press, 1933.
  This is the official history of Ch'ŏndogyo. It has been used as a major source of de-tailed, historical information, particularly for the Tonghak period (1860-1905). It is somewhat less useful on the period of Japanese control (1906-1945) because of the early date of publication and because of the political restrictions on full reporting of Ch'ŏndogyo activities during that period.

Ch'ŏndogyo Chŏngch'i Inyŏm (Political Ideas of Ch'ŏndogyo). Seoul: Posŏng Press, 1947.
  This brief post-World War II publication shows signs of hasty preparation, but provides the best available information on Ch'ŏndogyo's political-economic-cultural platform during the divided occupation of Korea after 1945. It also provides some checks on the censored statements in *Ch'ŏndogyo Ch'ang Kŏn Sa* on events during the Japanese period.

Chōsen Jimmei Jishō (Korean Biographical Dictionary). Seoul: Chōsen Shi Gakkai, 1927.

Chosŏn Chi Wiin (Eminent Koreans). Seoul: Kaebyŏksa, 1926.

Chung, Henry. *The Case of Korea*. New York: Revell, 1921.
  A useful English language source on the 1919 independence uprising.

Chung, Henry. *The Russians Came to Korea*. Washington: Korean Pacific Press.

Clark, Charles A. *Religions of Old Korea*. New York: Revell, 1932.
  Dr. Clark's work provides the most complete English language discussions of Ch'ŏndogyo as a religious cult. His quotations and commentaries provide helpful cross-checks on the official Ch'ŏndogyo sources.

Creel, Herrlee G. *Confucius, the Man and the Myth*. New York: John Day, 1949.

Curzon, (Lord) George N. *Problems of the Far East*. New York: Longmans, Green, 1896.

Cynn, Hugh Heung-wo. *The Rebirth of Korea*. New York: The Abingdon Press, 1920.

Dai Jimmei Jiten (The Great Dictionary of Personal Names). Tokyo: Heibonsha, 1953.
Dallet, Charles. *Histoire de l'église de Corée*. 2 Vols. Paris: Victor Palme, 1874.
Dallin, David J. *Soviet Russia and the Far East*. New Haven: Yale University Press, 1948.
Dallin, David J. *The Rise of Russia in the Far East*. New Haven: Yale University Press, 1949.
Dennett, Tyler. *Roosevelt and the Russo-Japanese War*. New York: Doubleday, Page, 1925.
Dennis, A. L. P. *Adventures in American Diplomacy, 1896-1906*. New York: Dutton, 1928.
Die Grosse Politik der Europaischen Kabinette, 1871-1914. Vol. XXXII. Berlin: 1924.
Gitovich, A., and B. Bursov. *North of the 38th Parallel*. Translated by George Leonof. Shanghai: Epoch Publishing Co., 1948.
Gooch and Temperley (eds.). *British Documents on the Origins of the War: 1898-1914*. Vols. I, IV, and VIII.
Han, Ch'ang-gyŏng, *Yŏkhak Wŏllon* (Study of the Book of Changes). Seoul: Hagusa, 1955.
    A good background study on the Confucian *Book of Changes*.
Han, U-gŭn, and Kim Ch'ŏl-chun, *Kuksa Kaeron* (General Discussion of Korean History). Seoul: Myŏnghaktang, 1954.
    This good general history of Korea provides useful background material on the periods leading up to the founding of Ch'ŏndogyo in 1860.
Hansard. Parliamentary Debates (Fourth Series). Vols. XXVI (1894), XXVII (1894), XXVIII (1894), and CXVII (1919).
Henderson, Gregory. "Chŏng Ta-san: A Study in Korea's Intellectual History," *The Journal of Asian Studies*, May, 1957, pp. 377-386.
Hong, I-sŏp, "Kabo Kyŏngjang Kwa Kidokkyo" (The 1894 Reforms and Christianity), *Sasanggye*, January, 1955, pp. 10-19.
Hsueh, Chung-san, and Yi, Ouyang. *A Sino-Western Calendar for Two Thousand Years, 1-2000 A.D.* Changsha: The Commercial Press, Ltd., 1940.
Hulbert, Homer B. *The History of Korea*. 2 Vols. Seoul: Methodist Publishing House, 1905.
    This is the standard English language history of Korea up to the period of Japanese control.
Hulbert, Homer B. "The Religion of the Heavenly Way," *Korea Review*, November, December, 1906.
Hummel, Arthur W. (ed.). *Eminent Chinese of the Ch'ing Period*. Washington: Government Printing Office, 1943.
Inaba, Iwakichi. "Chōsen Chūjin Kō" (A study of the Special Class in (Korea), *Tōa Keizai Kenkyū*, Vol. 17, No. 2.
Ishii, Toshio. "Tōgaku Shisō no Rekishiteki Tenkai" (Historical Development of Tonghak Thought), *Rekishigaku Kenkyū*, January, 1941, pp. 17-60.
Itō, Hirobumi (Prince). *Chōsen Kōshō Shiryō* (Source Materials on Relations with Korea). Tokyo: Hishō Ruisan Kankokai, 1936.
Japanese Government General in Korea. Statistical Study No. 42, *Chōsen No Ruiji Shukyō* (Psuedo-religions of Korea). Seoul: 1935.
Japanese Government General in Korea. *Chōsen no Dokuritsu Shisō Oyobi Undō* (Korean Independence Thought and Activities). Seoul: 1924.
Japanese Military Police Headquarters in Korea. *Taishō Hachinen Chōsen Shōyō Jiken Jōkyō* (A Report on the Korean Disturbance of 1919.).
    This official report (originally classified Secret) gives a thorough and generally factual account of the independence uprising, on the basis of police investigations.

Japanese Ministry of Foreign Affairs. *Nihon Gaikō Bunsho,* Vols. XXVI and XXVII. Tokyo: 1952.
These official documents contain the Tonghak petition to the King and Tonghak materials expressing opposition tó Christianity and foreigners in general.

Journal of Asiatic Studies. Seoul: Asiatic Research Center of Korea University, Vol. III, No. 1 (June, 1960) ff.
This scholarly journal has made available to the public for the first time the *Ilsŏngnok* (Court Diary) and the *Sŭngjŏngwŏn Ilgi* (Royal Secretariat Diary). Both contain official records of the trials of Chŏn Pong-jun and other captured rebel leaders.

Junkin, William M. "The Tong Hak," *Korean Repository,* Vol. II (1895), pp. 56-61.

Kaebyŏk (Creation), June, July, and September, 1920.
The editorials and articles in this official Ch'ŏndogyo periodical provide helpful insights into the Ch'ŏndogyo philosophy and program during the period of Japanese control.

Kang, Chae-ŏn. "Chōsen ni okeru Hōken Taisei no Kaitai to Nōmin Sensō" (The Breakdown of the Feudal System and the Farmers' Struggle in Korea), *Rekishigaku Kenkyū,* July, 1954, pp. 1-15; November, 1954, pp. 12-25.

Karl, Hongkee. "A Critical Evaluation of Modern Social Trends in Korea." Unpublished Ph.D. dissertation, Department of Comparative Religion, University of Chicago, 1934.

Kim, Sang-dŏk. *Chosŏn Tongnip Undong Sa* (History of the Korean Independence Movement). Seoul: Chosŏn Publication and Culture Co., 1946.
This is a standard history of the Korean independence movement, with particular emphasis on the 1919 uprising.

Kim, Sang-gi. *Tonghak Kwa Tonghak Nan* (Tonghak and the Tonghak Rebellion). Seoul: Taesŏng Press, 1947.
This is a major source for the Tonghak period of Ch'ŏndogyo. The author is an able, recognized historian who is, however, somewhat partial to the orthodox Tonghak leaders as opposed to the rebel element.

Kim, Tŭk-hwang. *Hanguk Sasang sa* (History of Korean Thought). Seoul: Namsandang, 1958.

Kim, Ul-han. "Ch'ŏndogyo Sŏngmyŏng ŭl Haemyŏng Ham" (Explaining the Ch'ŏndogyo Statement). Hanguk Ilbo, July 3, 1957, p. 4.
A justification of Christian cooperation with Ch'ŏndogyo in the 1919 uprising.

Kim, Yŏng-dŏk. "Silla, Koryŏ, Yijo Sahoe ŭi Tangye-jŏk Ch'ai-sŏng e Taehayŏ" (Concerning Class Differences in the Silla, Koryŏ, and Yi Dynasties). *Sasanggye,* February, 1955, pp. 10-24.

Ko, Kwŏn-sam. *Chōsen Seiji-shi Kō* (Outline of Korean Political History). Tokyo: Nagada Shoten, 1933.

Kyŏngguk Taejŏn (The Great Administrative Code). Seoul: Japanese Government General in Korea, 1934.

Langer, William L. (ed.). *An Encyclopedia of World History.* Boston: Houghton Mifflin, 1948.

MacNair, Harley Farnsworth. *Modern Chinese History, Selected Readings.* Shanghai: The Commercial Press, Ltd., 1933.

Malloy, W. M. (ed.). *Treaties, Conventions, etc.* Vol. I. Washington: Government Printing Office, 1910.

Mayers, William F. *The Chinese Reader's Manual.* Shanghai: Kelly and Walsh, 1924.

McCordock, R. Stanley. *British Far Eastern Policy, 1894-1900.* New York: Columbia University Press, 1931.

McKenzie, F. A. *Korea's Fight For Freedom.* New York: Revell, 1920.

Min T'ae-wan. *Kapsin Chŏngbyŏn Kwa Kim Ok-kyun* (The 1884 Incident and Kim Ok-kyun). Seoul: Kukche Munhwa Hyŏphoe, 1947.

Mitchell, Clyde C. *Final Report and History of the New Korea Company.* Seoul: Head-quarters, U. S. Army Military Government in Korea, National Land Admin-istration, 1948.

Nelson, M. Frederick. *Korea and the Old Orders in Eastern Asia.* Baton Rouge: Louisi-ana State University Press, 1945.

O, Chae-sik. *Hang-Il Sun'guk Uiyŏlsa Chŏn* (Biography of Martyred Anti-Japanese Patriots). Seoul: Aeguk Chŏngsin Sonyanghoe, 1957.

O, Chi-yŏng. *Tonghak Sa* (History of Tonghak). Seoul: Yŏngch'ang Sŏgwan, 1940.
     An important source on the Tonghak period, written by a recognized historian who was associated with the rebel leader, Chŏn Pong-jun, but retained the respect of the orthodox leaders and was able to mediate the dispute between the two factions.

O, Ik-che. "Sam-il Undong Kwa Wŏllam Sŏnsaeng" (The March First Movement and Wŏllam [Yi Sang-jae]). *Hanguk Ilbo,* July 8, 1957, p. 4.

Paek, Se-myŏng. "Kabo Kyŏngjang Kwa Ch'ŏndogyo Sasang" (The Reforms of 1894 and Ch'ŏndogyo Thought). *Sasanggye,* November, 1954, pp. 43-66.

Paik, L. George. *The History of Protestant Missions in Korea, 1832-1910.* Pyongyang: Union Christian College Press, 1929.

Pak, Un-sik. *Hanguk Tongnip Undong Chi Hyŏlsa* (The Bloody History of the Korean Independence Movement), Shanghai: Yusinsa, 1920.
     This standard history of the Korean independence movement was prepared under the auspices of the Korean Provisional Government, established in China after the 1919 uprising.

Rockhill, W. W. (ed.). *Treaties and Conventions With or Concerning China and Korea, 1894-1904.* Washington: Government Printing Office, 1904.

Rockhill, W. W. (Compiler). *Treaties, Conventions, Agreements, Ordinances, Etc., October, 1904-January, 1908.* Washington: Government Printing Office, 1908.

Rosen, Baron. *Forty Years of Diplomacy.* London: George Allen and Unwin, 1922.

Seoul Taehak Kuksa Yŏn'gu Sil (Korean History Research Center, Seoul National University). *Kuksa Kaesŏl* (Outline of Korean History). Seoul: Hongmungwan, 1952.

Shigada, Hiroshi. "Kyūrai no Chōsen Shakai no Rekishiteki Seikaku" (Old Korean Society and its Historical Characteristics). *Chōsen Gakuhō* No. 3, May 1952, p. 136.

Sin, T'ae-ak. "Sam-il Undong ŭi Chudong Inmul ŭn Nugu" (Who Was the Principal Individual in the March First Movement?). *Hanguk Ilbo,* July 10, 1957, p. 4.
     This article gives principal credit to the Ch'ŏndogyo leader, Ch'oe Rin.

Tonggyŏng Taejŏn. Seoul: Posŏng Press, 1947.
     This, the Ch'ŏndogyo "Bible," is the most authentic source for doctrinal pronounce-ments by the Ch'ŏndogyo founder, Ch'oe Che-u.

Tonghak Nan Kirok (Records of the Tonghak Rebellion). 2 vols. Seoul: Kuksa P'yŏnch'an Wiwŏnhoe (History Compilation Committee), 1960.
     The materials in these two volumes consist of original documents written in the years 1894 and 1895 and having some bearing on the Tonghak Rebellion of 1894. A large number of the documents are reports to the Korean Government from officials dispatched to southwestern Korea to investigate the uprising. Major emphasis is on developments of essentially local significance. The most useful of these materials is the court record of the trial of Chŏn Pong-jun and 27 other important Tonghak leaders.

U.S. Army Military Government in Korea, Department of Public Information, Bureau of Public Opinion. *Prominent Political Parties in South Korea and Their Tendencies.* Seoul: January, 1948.

U.S. Congress. *Congressional Record.* 66th Congress, 1st Session; 66th Congress, 2nd Session; 68th Congress, 1st Session; 68th Congress, 2nd Session.

U.S. Department of State. *Foreign Relations of the United States,* 1894, App. I; 1895; 1905; 1906; 1910.

U.S. Department of State. *The Conflict in Korea.* Publication 4266. Washington: Gov ernment Printing Office, 1951.

U.S. Department of State. *Korea, 1945 to 1948.* Publication 3305. Washington: Government Printing Office, 1948.

U.S. Department of State. *Korea's Independence.* Publication 2933. Washington: Government Printing Office, 1947.

U.S. Department of State. *United States Relations with China.* Washington: Government Printing Office, 1949.

Vinacke, Harold M. *A History of the Far East in Modern Times.* 4th edition. New York: Crofts, 1941.

Vladimir (Psued.) Z. Volpicelli. *The China-Japan War.* London: Sampson Low, Marston, 1896.

Wasson, Alfred W. *Church Growth in Korea.* New York: International Missionary Council, 1934.

Watanabe, Yoru. *Tendokyō to Jitenkyō* (Ch'ŏndogyo and Sich'ŏngyo). Seoul: publ. privately, 1919.

Weems, Clarence N., Jr. "The Korean Reform and Independence Movement (1881-1898)." Unpublished Ph.D. Dissertation, Columbia University (Faculty of Political Science), 1954.

This is a thorough, well-documented research study, using all available oriental and western language sources. This dissertation and much additional unpublished material by Dr. Weems covering earlier and later time periods have been referred to extensively in the preparation of the present study.

Wilbur, C. Martin. "Japan and the Korean Farmer," *Asia* Vol. XXV, No. 6 (June, 1935), pp. 394-397.

Wilkinson, W. H. *The Korean Government: Constitutional Changes, July 1894 to October 1895.* London: P.S. King and Son, 1897.

Yang, Key P., and Gregory Henderson. "An Outline History of Korean Confucianism," Parts I and II *Journal of Asian Studies,* November 1958 and February 1959.

Yarmolinsky, Abraham (trans. and ed.). *The Memoirs of Count Witte.* Garden City: Doubleday, Page, 1921.

Yi, Man-ch'ae. *Pyŏgwi P'yŏn* (Compilations of a Defense Against Heresy). Seoul: Kaebyŏksa, 1931.

Yi, Nŭng-hwa. *Chosŏn Kidokkyo Kŭp Oegyo Sa* (History of Korean Christianity and Diplomacy). Seoul: Kidokkyo Ch'angmunsa, 2 Vol. 1925.

Yi, Pyŏng-do. *Kuksa Taegwan* (General Survey of National History). Seoul: Tongjisa, 1949.

Yi, Pyŏng-do. *Tugye Chapp'il* (Miscellaneous Writings of Tugye [Yi Pyŏng-do]). Seoul: Ilchogak, 1956.

This work by Dean Yi Pyŏng-do is a principal source of information on the intense exploitation of Korean farmers during the latter part of the Yi Dynasty. This exploitation was one of the direct causes of the establishment of the Tonghak (Ch'ŏndogyo) movement and of the launching of the Tonghak Rebellion of 1894.

Yi, Pyŏng-do. "Toch'am e Taehan Il i ŭi Koch'al" (Some Studies on Toch'am, Omens, and Predictions). *Chintan Hakpo,* Vol. 10, March 1939, pp. 1-18.

Yi, Sang-baek. "Sŏŏl Kŭmgo Simal" (An Account of the Practice of Ostracism of th' Offspring of Concubines). Tongbang Hakchi, Vol. 1, pp. 159-330.

Yi, Sang-baek. "Ch'ilsŏ-ji Ok" (Record of the Criminal Case of the Seven Illegitimatι Sons). Tugye Yi Pyŏng-do Paksa Hoegap Kiryŏm Saŏp Wiwŏn Hoe (Committee foι the Commemoration of the Sixtieth Birthday of Dr. Yi Pyŏng-do). *Kiryŏm Non-ch'ong* (Commemorization Collection) Seoul: Ilchogak, 1956.

Yi, Sang-baek. *Yijo Kŏnguk ŭi Yŏn'gu* (A Study of the Founding of the Yi Dynasty).

Seoul: Ulyu Publishing Co., 1949.

Yi, Sang-guk. *Hanguk Munhwa Sa Kaegwan* (An Outline Korean Cultural History). Seoul: Hyŏndaesa, 1955.

Yi, Sŏn-gun. *Hwarangdo Yŏn'gu* (A Study of Korean Knighthood). Seoul: Haedong Cultural Press, 1949.

Yi, Ton-hwa. *In Nae Ch'ŏn ui Youi* (Essentials of In Nae Ch'ŏn). Seoul: Ch'ŏndogyo Central Headquarters, 1924.
    This is a basic Ch'ŏndogyo doctrinal work by the foremost modern Ch'ŏndogyo theologian and philosopher.

Yu, Hong-nyŏl. *Chosŏn Ch'ŏnju Kyohoe Sa* (The History of Korean Catholicism). Vol. 1. Seoul: Chosŏn Ch'ŏnju Kyohoe Sungyo-ja Hyŏnyang Hoe, 1949.

Zabriskie, Edward H. *American-Russian Rivalry in the Far East*. Philadelphia: University of Pennsylvania Press, 1946.

INDEX